T·H·E
ENVIRONMENTAL
FACTOR

T · H · E
ENVIRONMENTAL
FACTOR

ITS IMPACT ON THE FUTURE OF THE WORLD ECONOMY AND YOUR INVESTMENTS

MICHAEL SILVERSTEIN

Longman Financial Services Publishing
a division of Longman Financial Services Institute, Inc

The contents of this book is printed on acid-free paper.

While a great deal of care has been taken to provide accurate and current information, the ideas, suggestions, general principles and conclusions presented in this book are subject to local, state and federal laws and regulations, court cases and any revisions of same. The reader is thus urged to consult legal counsel regarding any points of law—this publication should not be used as a substitute for competent legal advice.

Executive Editor: Kathleen A. Welton
Project Editor: Ronald J. Liszkowski
Interior Design: Mary Kushmir
Cover Design: Anthony Russo

© 1990 by Michael Silverstein

Published by Longman Financial Services Publishing
a division of Longman Financial Services Institute, Inc.

Printed in the United States of America.

90 91 92 10 9 8 7 6 5 4 3 2

Library of Congress Cataloging-in-Publication Data

Silverstein, Michael, 1941–
    The environmental factor : its impact on the future of the world economy and your investments / Michael Silverstein.
        p.   cm.
    Bibliography: p.
    Includes index.
    ISBN 0-088462-911-2
    1. Investments. 2. Finance, Personal. 3. United States—Economic policy—1981– 4 Environmental policy—United States. I. Title.
HG4521.S567   1989
338.09--dc20   89-12589
                                                                CIP

TABLE OF CONTENTS

Preface   ix

PART I.   THE ENVIRONMENTAL FACTOR
          AND THE ECONOMY   1

Chapter 1.   The Big Picture   3
   A Rising Concern • On the American Front •
   Living with Less • Working Solutions •
   Beyond Wall Street

Chapter 2.   The Great Environmental Regulation
             Machine   23
   The Seeds of Environmentalism •
   Government Involvement Grows • State and
   Local Governments Step In • The Laws •
   The Consequences of Regulation

Chapter 3.   An Environment-Shaped Economy   41
   Down on the Farm • Of Transport and
   Energy • Insurance and Banking •
   Economy-Wide Concerns

PART II.   THE ENVIRONMENTAL FACTOR
           AND INVESTING   63

Chapter 4.   The Environmental Factor
             and Health Care   65
   In Context • The Economic Response

**Chapter 5.   The Environmental Factor
and Real Estate**   **71**
Beginning with the Family Home • The Cost
to the Homeowner • Self-Defense for Home
Buyers

Chapter 6.   The Environmental Factor and Stocks   **87**
Wall Street's Heightened Interest • The
Basics • The Bane of the Industry •
Secondary Plays • Environmental Self-Help •
Peripheral Investing Vision • Power From
the Sun • The Hedge

Chapter 7.   The Environmental Factor and Bonds   **109**
The Bond Fund Dilemma • The
Environment's Role • The Junk Flows In •
More Junk • A Different Approach

**Chapter 8.   The Environmental Factor
and Commodities**   **119**
Another Disaster to Consider • The Effect
Spreads • The Hedge

**PART III.   THE ENVIRONMENTAL FACTOR
AND THE WORKPLACE**   **125**

**Chapter 9.   The Environmental Factor and
Executive Planning**   **127**
Compliance by Convenience • Consciousness-
Raising • The Buck Stops Here • The
Earthquake Factor • The Bright Side •
Environmental Marketing • Siting the New
Plant

Contents

Chapter 10. **The Environmental Factor and Employment Opportunities**   **143**
Employment Possibilities • A New Growth Sector • Educational Opportunities • What the Employment Numbers Mean

Chapter 11. **The Environmental Factor and Entrepreneurship**   **155**
Environmental Self-Defense • The Food We Eat • The Clothes We Wear • Where We Live • Recycling • Compost Recycling • Designer Garbage?

PART IV. **THE ENVIRONMENTAL FACTOR AND THE FUTURE**   **171**

Chapter 12. **The Environmental Factor and Economic Forecasting**   **173**
The Voice of the Press

Chapter 13. **Who Will Pay the Environmental Tab?**   **179**
Fudging the Numbers • Acknowledging the Problem May Get Worse • Waste Inflation Run Amok • Increase of Sites • Potato Passing • Hot Potato • Another Hot Potato • And Another Hot Potato • Hot Potato, Again! • Taking Sides

Chapter 14. **Environmental Alchemy and Personal Transformation**   **199**
Alchemy Put to Use • The Way Things Are

Appendix   **207**
    Residential Real Estate Checklist • Stock
    Checklist • Bonds Checklist

Bibliography   **211**

Index   **223**

PREFACE

Many books are being written about the environment. Many are being written about the economy. This volume is about the relationship of the two. More specifically, it is about how environmental deterioration is shaping the workings of this country's economic system.

The book has a strong moral bias because in today's world, it is impossible not to appreciate the moral consequences of economic activities as they affect natural systems—even if one were inclined to do so. But this is not just an environmentalist's "cry from the heart." Indeed, the economic case here is so compelling, one could ignore the bias completely and still derive benefit from the reading.

What I attempt to show in these pages is that a very strong economic rationale now exists for environmentally sound behavior. It is a rationale that has important implications for investors, for company executives, for those seeking promising careers, for those looking forward to running their own businesses—for everyone, in fact, who is an active participant in our economic system.

At first glance, such a fusion of environmentalism and old-fashioned capitalism may seem gimmicky or even

Pollyannaish. Everyone would like to help protect and preserve the environment, of course. But why, one might ask, if opportunities in this realm are so good, have so many successful enterprises polluted over the years and so few been involved in pollution-fighting?

The answer is that this fusion of environmentalism and profit potential is a relatively new development. It required decades of legislation and regulation to take hold in ways that have finally jelled to make formerly profitable polluting activities much less profitable and formerly "utopian" approaches to economic matters quite lucrative.

To phrase this in a totally amoral way: You could have made a good buck in the past ignoring the environment or even helping to destroy the environment. You will make an even better buck in the future helping to clean up the mess.

While certainly a positive thing in many ways, this view is in no wise optimistic. An individual who suffers a coronary becomes much more aware of the need for proper diet and regular exercise. Though better diet and improved physical regimen are good things, however, the heart trouble that provoked the change of habits is not only frightening but also hints at possible worse things to come.

The same mechanics exist in the new environment-economy relationship. As a society, we have so damaged and overloaded natural systems that the luxury of polluting we abused (and enjoyed) for so many years is no longer an option compatible with satisfying primary human needs for drinkable water, breathable air, and safe places in which to live and work.

Thus, there is little joy in the environment-shaped economy that is fast evolving in the United States. It is an extremely disturbing new fact of life that no one planned, willed or wanted. It is, nonetheless, something we must all learn to live with.

This book, then, is not a plea for more environmentally responsible behavior. Nor is it a tract designed for environmentalists seeking additional ammunition to use against "Corporate America." It is a guide to sensible economic behavior dictated by changed circumstances. It is an outline for coping with a nasty new set of realities that can no longer be ignored.

Most of the data used in writing this book come from periodicals, trade group and government studies, annual reports, speeches, newsletters and other "contemporary" sources. (See the bibliography for a full list of sources.) There is no other way to handle this topic at present. No real book literature exists in this field yet because until recently, people who wrote about the environment tended not to focus on economic themes, while those who wrote about economics tended not to focus on ecosystems.

Some of the facts on government environmental policies in the following pages may therefore be familiar to careful readers of news dailies and weeklies. Some of the descriptions of real estate trends will be known to those who follow the real estate trade press. People who read specialized bond and commodity publications, management journals, the recycling press, annual reports from firms in the environmental services industries, etc., will find some statistics and notions in the following pages that they may have come across previously.

What I have sought to do with this material is to put it into a slightly different context—to organize it in ways that bring the economic aspects of environmental decline into sharper focus. From this new perspective, *The Environmental Factor* can be seen as a critical element in international developments such as the present overhaul of the Soviet economy, in domestic economic problems such as the burgeoning American health-care crisis, and in a host of personal asset management and career decisions, ranging from which stocks to buy to where to locate the new corporate headquarters.

A number of persons were very helpful in making this book possible. I would especially like to thank Kay Wood for her invaluable insights and editorial suggestions and Jon Silverstein for his assistance in pinpointing key ideas that ultimately evolved into chapters.

Michael Silverstein
Philadelphia
1989

PART I

The Environmental Factor and the Economy

CHAPTER 1

The Big Picture

Inflation, trade patterns and debtor-lender relations will all be important in shaping U.S. and world economies in the 1990s. The most important force shaping tomorrow's economics, however, will be environmental deterioration. To a large extent, this is already the case.

Until recently, people concerned with environmental decline usually focused on its ecological ramifications. They pointed at man-made pollution that is causing the greatest mass extinction of species since the dinosaurs became extinct 65 million years ago.

The impact of pollution on quality of life has also been a long-time theme of environmentalists. The disappearance of pure water, fresh air and unspoiled outdoor space in which to enjoy both has long been cited as too great a price to pay for material progress.

The grave economic consequences of environmental decline, however, have been overlooked or slighted by both the environmentalist community and the general public. An appreciation of the importance of the economy-environment relationship has been slow to evolve.

Professional economists have done little to foster awareness in this field. Few factored environmental decline into their thinking for the simple reason that in purely economic terms, there seemed little reason to do so until quite recently.

For a long time people have enjoyed a relatively free ride with respect to pollution. An accommodating Mother Nature cleaned up our wastes gratis. Serious cases of pollution tended to be local and temporary. Given enough time, the seas, the rivers and the winds made everything right.

That is no longer true. So many natural systems have been sickened by human wastes that they can no longer function as efficient "cheap sweepers." Increasingly, the costs of people-caused pollution and contamination are having to be borne by people. Thus, for purely economic reasons, the *environmental factor* has become a filter through which future economic development must pass.

At the root of this changed situation are two revolutions, one demographic, the other technological. The world's population has increased fivefold in the past 100 years. It has more than doubled since 1950.

More and more of these people know about and hope to share in the fruits of industrial culture—a culture based on the use of some 60,000 complex, often environmentally toxic, substances. Industrial pollution, once restricted to a few nations in Europe and the New World, has now spread to all parts of the globe.

A Rising Concern

Before the summer of 1988 the economic benefits of this vast assault on the environment were deemed worth its cost in quality of life by most people and their governments. Only lately have the full economic consequences of pollution, as well as these quality-of-life costs, begun to be fully understood.

This new perception is rapidly taking hold everywhere as people see their prosperity challenged in tandem with the decline of their natural surroundings. Severely impaired ecological systems in the Eastern Bloc illustrate this point clearly.

The less-aggressive foreign policy currently being pursued by Mikhail Gorbachev's Soviet Union is at least partially due to environmentally linked economic troubles. Chernobyl and its costly medical and psychological aftermath come to mind immediately in this regard. But the world's most devastating nuclear accident is only one symptom of a far more pervasive malady.

For decades, Soviet leadership has sacrificed air, water and soil quality to industrial development, building heavy manufacturing facilities without smokestack filters and recklessly dumping raw filth into inland waterways. The economic results of this shortsightedness are now becoming apparent.

There have been dozens of costly man-made ecological disasters in the Soviet Union in recent years. The cotton crops around the Aral Sea are being threatened by pesticides and defoliants. The results of bungled handling of projects around the huge, man-made Kuban Sea in the southern part of the country are threatening the livelihood of hundreds of thousands of people, and will likely cost the equivalent of billions of dollars to repair. A progressively more degraded national landscape throughout the country is eroding worker morale and productivity in scores of industries.

The appeal of Black Sea beaches for vacationers is fading because of water contamination. Soviet nuclear vessels sometimes cannot even dock in their own ports because of on-board radioactive leaks. Many long-time favorites in the Russian diet, such as Volga caviar, are disappearing as sturgeon succumb to pollution.

The economic toll of long-term environmental disdain is even more extensive in the Eastern Bloc satellite nations. Much of Estonia's drinking water supply, for example, is now endangered by local mining operations. Freshwater fishing in such rivers as the Oder is just a memory. From Dresden to Prague, the exquisite public statuary that once attracted millions of tourists is being destroyed by acids in the atmosphere.

Poland is the most extreme example of Eastern Bloc environmental deterioration. Whole Polish villages have had to be evacuated because of local environmental conditions. Some 30 percent of the country's entire population now lives in areas the government itself categorizes as environmental disaster zones.

By 1984, an estimated 71 percent of Poland's drinking water had been classified as undrinkable. Simply to cope with (though not correct) the effects of past environmental errors will cost the Polish economy the equivalent of about 10 percent of Poland's entire gross national product this year.

Western Europe is suffering less environmentally caused economic trauma than the eastern European countries. But here, too, the costs of pollution are beginning to be serious drains on national economies.

The same acid rain destroying trees in Czechoslovakia and East Germany has killed an estimated 50 percent of the forests in parts of the Federal Republic of Germany. Air-pollution–related damage of all kinds in western Europe was estimated to exceed $3 billion annually as early as 1983. In northern parts of the United Kingdom and southern areas of the Iberian peninsula sulfur dioxide levels are regularly greater than 180 percent of World Health Organization guidelines.

A thousand miles of Adriatic Sea coastline has lost its fisheries and is fast losing much of its annual tourist trade. On the other end of the continent, the North Sea has become industrialized Europe's sewer, with even more negative economic consequences for inhabitants of the region. To combat local pollution, the Dutch government has been obliged to inaugurate an environmental program that will cost the country more than $8 billion annually.

Britons have found their butter tainted with mercury (a result of industrial dumping near food-producing regions). They are also becoming aware that many of their cities are infested with rats because Victorian-vintage sewer systems can no longer cope with the urban wastes pouring into them, and government is unwilling or unable to spend to replace the piping.

In Ireland, following a gold strike, some of the country's last untainted streams and lakes are threatened by mining-related cyanide contamination. Most of Ireland is massively contaminated by industrial and agricultural runoffs.

The only thing that keeps Naples from being the filthiest port in Europe (with all the nasty economic side effects such a title implies) is the Spanish port of Bilbao, whose citizens have contrived to make their own prime economic resource environmentally inhospitable.

A long-time favorite practice of Europeans—dumping their toxic wastes in the old colonial lands of Africa—has gone out of favor in the wake of scandals involving vessels of Dutch and Italian registry. The cost of domestically incinerating a greater percentage of the 22 million tons of hazardous waste produced each year by western Europeans will therefore constitute a much larger business overhead expense in Common Market countries in years to come.

It currently costs about $2,000 a ton to incinerate such waste in Europe. It used to cost only $20 a ton to dump it into landfills in western Africa.

If the prospective economic consequences of spreading pollution seem frightening in Europe, they appear far more frightening for Third World countries. The entire economic base of the sub-Sahara region of Africa, traditionally built around agriculture and pasturage, is being undermined by overpopulation and its associated environmental damage. Such natural and economic resources as Lake Victoria are being contaminated and overfished. Collectively, the food output of the 45 nations in this region has exceeded population growth just *once* since 1970.

Similar factors are at work in Madagascar, where 80 percent of the economically all-important forests have been destroyed in recent decades. In our own hemisphere, a kindred process is observable in desperately impoverished Haiti. Once the economic jewel of the French overseas empire, Haiti today is an environmental disaster zone and an economic basket case.

Many of the most important natural resources of Asia are yielding to the same pressures. In China, rapid industrialization and heavy dependence on coal are poisoning the air in cities and raising health care costs dramatically.

In India, massive destruction of forests is causing fuel shortages and fuel price inflation in many parts of the country. Destruction of the Himalayan forests is causing ever more serious flooding downstream in Bangladesh.

Hardwood forests from Malaysia to Borneo are being overcut, ruining the hunting on which local people depend. Nepal and Sri Lanka have lost larger percentages of their wooded resources in recent years than any other countries on earth. In Thailand, where trees covered two-thirds of the land in the 1950s, they now cover just 20 percent, and hundreds of Thais are dying in floods each year because water runoff is no longer restrained by woodlands.

An estimated 95 percent of the coral reefs that provide a living for thousands of fishermen in the Philippines have been damaged by cyanide contamination. The magnificent forests of Palawan in the Philippines are being systematically overlogged and destroyed.

The destruction of the Brazilian rain forest, estimated at 100,000 square kilometers a year (an area equal to two percent of the entire region) has enormous negative effects on fishing, farming, rubber-tapping and scores of other indigenous industries, as well as a host of negative consequences for the international economy as a whole.

The World Resources Institute estimates that 20 percent of the world's population is "periodically disrupted by flooding, fuelwood shortages, soil and water degradation, and reduced agricultural production caused directly or indirectly by the loss of tropical-forest cover." What sets Brazil's Amazon policies apart when it comes to this pandemic trend is only their scope.

Perhaps a quarter to a half of all new carbon added to the earth's atmosphere annually, with its contribution to the increasing greenhouse effect, results from forest burning. Much of this burning takes place in the Brazilian Amazon where in 1988 more than 48,000 square miles, an area larger than Pennsylvania, was put to the torch.

Brazil's experiment in environmental suicide is the best-known Latin-American example of ecological short-sightedness with serious economic spinoffs. It is far from being a unique policy on that continent, however. The health care costs of excessive air pollution are well documented, and such costs are spiraling in virtually every major city of Latin America.

In Santiago, Chile, smog has gotten so bad that planes periodically fly over the city spraying detergent in hopes of reducing levels of pollution in the air. In Mexico City, schoolchildren were given an emergency one-month vacation in the winter of 1988 because air inversions combined with local air pollution made it too dangerous for them to walk to their schools. U.S. diplomats stationed in Mexico City are warned not to bring their children to this posting.

Air is not the only natural element suffering deterioration in financially strapped Mexico. In recent years, the northern part of the country, bordering on California and Texas, has experienced something of a manufacturing boom as Japanese and American manufacturers have moved in to take advantage of cheap labor and ready access to U.S. markets. The environmental spinoff of this boom is that factories making cheap electronic products for export are now dumping thousands of tons of toxic chemicals annually in the area, and this material is beginning to threaten local aquifers.

Thus, one economic cost of Mexico's tainted air is a less-well-educated population of schoolchildren. Another is a loss of tourism. In addition, the industrial boom in Mexico's northern provinces and the resulting contamination of drinking water will almost certainly increase national health care expenditures in future decades.

Just as the northern areas of Mexico that abut the United States are among Mexico's most polluted, the southern border areas of Canada, which meet the U.S. and where some 90 percent of Canadians live, are also long-time pollution zones. The destruction of Canada's Pacific Coast rain forests could well have economic—if not ecological—consequences rivaling those in Amazonia.

Even areas of the globe without human inhabitants are feeling the effect of man-made pollution. The Antarctic has long been a breeding ground for countless fish and bird species, many of which are important links in natural food chains.

An oil spill when an Argentine ship broke up in rough seas in early 1989 was the first direct pollution threat to this priceless resource. A few weeks later, oil from a leaking Peruvian vessel killed thousands of penguins in this same region.

Discovery of a hole in the ozone layer above the Antarctic, first reported in the mid-1980s, was followed by a report of a similar hole above the Arctic. Higher levels of solar radiation now penetrate to both of the world's polar regions, and represent a costly threat not only to commercial aquatic species but also to the health of human inhabitants of Greenland and northern Canada.

The southern Arctic has also been contaminated by oil exploration and drilling. A huge spill off Valdez, Alaska, in March 1989 not only played havoc with local herring fishermen but threatens dozens of other livelihoods in this magnificent scenic area—not to mention the future prospects for another generation of oil drillers.

The international aspects of environmental deterioration are increasingly evident. And the international community has been moving in recent years to face these concerns.

In 1987, 31 nations signed an agreement in Montreal committing manufacturers within their borders to cut production of ozone-damaging chemicals by 50 percent by the year 2000. In early 1989, after more data on ozone damage were available, representatives of 112 nations met in London and agreed to cut this production by 85 percent within the same time frame.

The United Nations declared its first "Environmental Sabbath" in June 1988. The International Union for Conservation of Nature and Natural Resources, which first met in New Delhi, India, in early 1989, recommended higher taxes on gasoline and other fossil fuels to pay for environmental cleanup costs. The U.N. Environmental Program put the final touches on a transnational treaty governing the handling of toxic wastes in early 1989. The treaty was signed by representatives of more than 100 nations. In June 1989, environmental ministers of the European Community voted tough and expensive new car emission standards that will go into effect in 1992.

On the American Front

Given the vast and growing impact of environmental deterioration on economies around the world, it is not surprising that the same phenomenon should be increasingly evident in the United States. There is hardly a field of economic endeavor in this country that is not beginning to feel the impact of environmental decline, if it is not, in fact, already suffering the consequences of that decline.

Among the things presently pushing up domestic inflation rates are "passthrough" costs of companies' compliance with ever-more-stringent environmental regulations. Taxes, especially at the city and county levels, are rising steeply to cover soaring expenses associated with trash collection and disposal. The enormous environmental liabilities of literally thousands of corporations threaten the dividends and jobs of millions of investors and workers.

Noting just a few *estimated* costs of cleaning up the most serious environmental damages in this country hints at the economic magnitude of this problem. To render areas around the military's 12 nuclear weapons plants safe from radioactive and toxic wastes will require upward of $50 billion. To make 45 government nuclear facilities (including these plants) safe might require $200 billion over a 30-year period.

The collection and disposal of solid wastes now costs Americans $20 billion a year, and could cost at least $30 billion a year when more stringent laws like those recently enacted by New York state come into effect. The bill for keeping our present drinking water purification systems operating over the next five years will run to between $75 and $85 billion. Complying with existing air pollution standards now costs utilities and manufacturers some $25 to $33 billion annually, and this could jump another

$19 billion a year if President Bush's clean-air proposals, made in June 1989, are put into effect.

American industry has a hazardous-waste bill that has been estimated at between $100 to $700 billion. The Environmental Protection Agency (EPA) has identified 29,000 contaminated sites around the country, and state governments have an even larger number on their own lists.

To comply with new regulations related to long-term release of toxic substances will cost business some 13 million man-hours a year. About 25 percent of this country's 3.5 million small businesses are affected by new rules on workplace toxics. These businesses will have to spend an average of $5,000 to $10,000 each to achieve compliance.

Anyway one looks at it, no matter how conservative the computation, it becomes clear that hundreds of billions—perhaps trillions—of dollars will have to be spent in the United States during the next decades on the most basic of needs: keeping air breathable, water drinkable, and the places where people live and work fit for human habitation. It is inconceivable that expenditures this huge will not to a large extent determine the overall outlines of the general economy.

Over the long term, the transformation of American society and its economic institutions into a more environmentally sound configuration could trigger whole new generations of prosperity. In scope and cost, the change-over might be compared to the one that took us from a pre-industrial to a fully industrialized nation. As a positive side effect, a transformation of this magnitude would certainly provide enormous opportunities to exercise the country's indigenous entrepreneurial spirit.

In the near future, however, the consequences of redesigning and rebuilding production methods made obsolete by their incompatibility with the environment will cause a great deal of economic dislocation and pain. To put this more simply: To preserve the natural resources on which life depends, huge amounts of capital that might otherwise go into personal consumption must go instead into redressing past environmental damage and retooling for a safer future.

Living with Less

In other words, to survive, we will have to live poorer for years to come. Beyond that, we will also have to live less freely. Traditional property rights, such as building where one likes and what one likes, will be impinged by environmental factors. So, too, will scores of the most mundane personal rights, like driving in smoggy weather and holding outdoor barbecues when certain atmospheric conditions prevail.

This model of the American future is totally contrary to the philosophy that animated the Reagan years, when "development" was all-paramount and was often realized at the expense of the environment. Such a philosophy is now recognizable as an environmental (and economic) shell game—even by Mr. Reagan's Republican successor.

It also differs from the model long employed by environmental groups. For decades the environmentalist argument has been that preservation and conservation were more important than economic progress. Love of nature was held up as the preferable alternative to love of material progress.

The new reality, that sound economics and good environmental policies are synonymous, is just starting to permeate the environmental community. The idea that love of nature has become largely extraneous as a rationale for environmental protection at a time when the very survival of humankind is threatened by environmental decline, and that nature-haters as well as nature-lovers now have good reason to be strong environmentalists, has also been slow to sink in. The increasingly obvious fact that forced conformity to environmentally sound norms has many nasty social and political implications has hardly been acknowledged, much less addressed, by established environmental groups.

The major impediment to achieving an environmentally viable economy, however, is not the outmoded philosophies or lagging perceptions among activists who have not yet exchanged ideological environmentalism for a more up-to-date variety. It is the bedrock question of who will underwrite the costs of the great transformation. Even amid all the recent signs that we are becoming aware of the horrors we have inflicted on natural systems, there remains a persistent belief (and hope) among many individuals and institutions that the expense of making things right can be palmed off on *other* individuals and institutions.

The federal government is an active participant in this charade. Caught in a budgetary squeeze abetted by the political unpopularity of new taxes, Congress and the administration pass comprehensive water and toxic-waste cleanup measures, then underfund programs and sequester money already funded. As part of the "New Federalism," Washington also ducks its responsibilities in this realm by assigning them to state and local governments.

These governments, unfortunately, face their own budget crises and lack the financial resources to do the job. In many cases, their power to borrow money for environment-related projects has been crippled by a slump in the municipal bond market, brought about by changes mandated by the 1986 Tax Reform Act.

Governments at all levels are doing their best to shift the burden of environmental cleanup to the private sector, with laws mandating costly remedies for past and present environmental sins and stiff fines and penalties for failure to comply. Industry, in turn, is trying to transfer the load to insurers or pass it along to consumers in the form of higher prices for goods and services. With increasing frequency, industry's response to a serious environmental claim is bankruptcy.

Ultimately, of course, the costs of cleaning up our national environment cannot be allocated to a single sector of the economy but must come out of everybody's pockets. Whether the chosen mechanism to achieve this end is increased taxation, bigger quasi-taxes packaged as "user fees," higher insurance rates, more expensive retail prices for products or a combination of all these approaches is largely irrelevant.

Unfortunately for the environment, arguments over who pays the bill, rather than how best to get on with the job, are now the core issue for government, the business establishment and many other large institutions when addressing environmental concerns. Until these entities evolve beyond the debate and litigation stage, much of the environmental load must be borne by individuals.

Working Solutions

It is possible that government and other American institutions will never be able to rise to the environmental challenge, as we discuss in a later chapter. In consensus societies like Japan, institutions, once reoriented, are highly effective means of revolutionary change. The Green Movement in Germany and the Netherlands suggests that certain European political systems may also have the potential to cope institutionally with enormous environmental problems.

In this country, the combination of vested interest intransigence, political systems paralyzed by outmoded ideologies and courts that delay interminably even the most needed actions holds little promise when it comes to addressing vital environmental matters. Even if such institutions do, eventually, come together on these issues, the delay could be disastrous.

In the interim, much can and must be accomplished by individuals. In fact, by practicing the "market environmentalism" described in this book and employing the environmental factor in more and more personal economic decisions, one can play a significant role in a vital social process, at the same time becoming more fiscally secure.

One can view market environmentalism as a kind of inverted Gresham's Law. Just as Sir Thomas Gresham in the sixteenth century noted that bad money drives good money out of circulation, market environmentalism has the positive effect of driving bad environmental policies "out of circulation" by making them less profitable.

Market environmentalism is already a significant economic force in this country. It is practiced by millions of American consumers when shopping in supermarkets. They buy biodegradable trash bags instead of plastic varieties with 400-year dump lives. They buy loose fresh produce instead of packaged fruits and vegetables so as not to add to the national solid-waste pool.

American consumers use their buying power in other ways to make environmental statements. In the wake of large oil or chemical spills, they boycott certain service stations or stop using the credit cards of offending companies.

Another form of market environmentalism is practiced on Wall Street. A number of mutual funds that apply "ethical investing" or "socially responsible" criteria to pick stocks for their portfolios have become quite popular since the first one appeared in the mid-1970s. Many college, religious and local government pension funds, which collectively have hundreds of billions of dollars to invest, also use these criteria today when making their selec-

17

tions. One ethical measure most apply is the environmental practices of companies under consideration.

The term *environmental factor*, as used in this book, however, is not just another term for ethical investing. It is an entirely different approach to asset management. The environmental factor deals exclusively with the relationship of an economic entity to the environment, without consideration of how that entity relates to South Africa, women's issues, minority rights, etc. It is less "ethical" and more pragmatic, in the sense that it does not simply shun companies with imperfect environmental records but also considers the economic implications of their overall operations.

The overriding aim of ethical investors is to avoid being tainted without losing too much capital appreciation or dividends in consequence. The overriding aim of people using the environmental factor is to actively promote environmental protection and preservation in ways that promote personal benefits to the greatest extent possible.

The decision about whether to invest in waste-handling companies illustrates these distinctions. Most ethical investors now take the position that because such firms are frequently cited for violations and fined by the government, they are not fit investment vehicles. Those using the environmental factor, on the other hand, while never condoning legal infractions, would probably conclude that because some violations are an inevitable part of the waste-handling business, it is a company's total impact (positive and negative) on the environment that is important. Therefore, to refuse to invest in a firm that pollutes in any way at all simply removes capital from the environmental cleanup market.

Just as the environmental factor is not synonymous with ethical investing, it is quite different from Wall Street's currently popular "environmental investing." The distinction here is mainly one of scope.

To most brokers on Wall Street, environmental investing means buying shares in a few dozen publicly traded pollution-control or environmental services. In this book, the environmental factor is used to evaluate not only Wall Street's burners and buriers, haulers and testers, solid-waste handlers and hazardous-waste collectors but also to evaluate a far larger spectrum of companies that people wishing to invest in "the environment" might well like to consider, including Fortune 500 firms with fast-expanding environmental services divisions or affiliates.

Of far greater significance, the environmental factor can be used to explore the environmental sensitivity and exposure of both large and small companies in virtually all sectors of the economy. A basic premise of this book is that anyone who does not employ this tool in evaluating possible investments in such industries as petrochemicals, utilities, insurance, transportation, banking, agribusiness, health care, etc., is simply missing the boat in terms of how these industries will perform in years to come.

Beyond Wall Street

The environmental factor has many important applications beyond as well as within the stock market. It is a valuable tool in judging the merits of such investments as bonds, commodities and real estate. It is of increasing importance to those looking for employment and entrepreneurial opportunities. It is becoming an indispensable element of overall business management and planning.

With respect to bond investments, the environmental factor has considerable worth when it comes to gauging future ratings risks to both corporate and municipal issues. If a utility cannot operate a nuclear facility because of environmental concerns, the worth of its bond debt is affected. If a municipality is hit by court-ordered environmental compliance orders it cannot meet, the ratings of its paper are threatened.

To apply the environmental factor to real estate, consider what a house is worth if it is discovered to be near a Times Beach or a Love Canal; what sort of resale value there is in a commercial building with radon in the basement or asbestos wrapped around the piping; and how complex it is in many parts of the country to get the "environmental bill of health" needed to begin a real estate development project.

In the employment realm, the number of career slots opening for both environmental tradespeople and professionals is phenomenal. In the entrepreneurial realm, this segment of the economy is the place to look today to build a new business. In the managerial realm, heightened awareness of the relationship of the environment to one's company is fast becoming a key to future advancement within many business organizations.

The usefulness of the environmental factor in making personal financial and professional decisions in years to come would be hard to exaggerate. In the breadth of its application, one might compare it to the tax factor that has long been vital in many kinds of economic decision-making or to the energy factor that played much the same role in the late 1970s.

For years, no sophisticated person would consider purchasing real property without considering the tax aspects of the deal. Between 1973 and 1981, from the Arab oil embargo to the unraveling of OPEC, it would have been equally odd for this same sophisticated individual not to ask how an investment matched up with the country's changed energy fortunes.

The primary difference between the environmental factor and these other factors—at least from money-management and career perspectives—is that tax policies and energy costs are susceptible to relatively easy human manipulation, whereas our present environmental troubles are not.

Congress reforms the Tax Code, and out go scores of tax shelters whose appeal influenced people's handling of money. An oil cartel loses its cohesiveness, and the fear of energy price rises immediately becomes less important in determining where capital migrates.

The state of world and national environmental systems cannot, unfortunately, be altered so easily. Even if all forms of new pollution were miraculously and suddenly to stop, the cumulative effects of past pollution would still require many years and huge capital expenditures to correct.

Thus, to a disturbing degree, as environmental deterioration increasingly becomes the most important force shaping the economy, the environmental factor becomes the most important key to personal and corporate financial survival. The next chapter considers the regulatory mechanism that links the environment to the economy.

CHAPTER 2

The Great Environmental Regulation Machine

The Reagan Administration was not noted for its zeal in protecting the environment. It would be incorrect, however, to say that government environmental regulation of business and industry waned in the 1980s.

A more accurate description of what happened in this period is that overall federal involvement in this field broadened considerably, while enforcement of certain specific environmental mandates tapered off. A sharp increase in regulation by many states, a dramatically heightened concern with environment-related matters by cities and counties and some key decisions by the courts more than compensated for any slackness on the federal level.

If steadily rising populations and technological growth are the chief causes of environmental deterioration, growing government regulation is the chief medium by which society seeks to check this deterioration. Understanding a bit about past and present environmental regulation is, therefore, important to people who wish to employ the environmental factor in their own economic lives.

The Seeds of Environmentalism

Protecting natural resources and beauty is a well-established tradition in this country. For most of our history, however, it was largely a personal and local matter, involving successful individuals acting to perpetuate their memories by donating large tracts of unspoiled lands (with instructions to keep it that way) to townships, foundations and educational institutions.

The "conservancy movement" that evolved out of this practice was very active by the end of the 19th century. It is still one of the chief protectors of America's natural heritage, removing almost 400,000 acres from free market development in 1988 alone.

Government moved into this field strongly at the beginning of the present century. Part of this new activism was motivated by a strong love of the land among public officials. Part expressed a desire to preserve fishing and hunting grounds. Part grew from the realization that if such resources as woodlands were not properly managed, they would one day stop producing valuable timber. The U.S. Department of the Interior and its state counterparts are the legacy of this "first-wave" official environmentalism.

The thing that primarily sets off Teddy Roosevelt-style conservationism from modern environmentalism is that the former was limited in its geographic and regulatory horizons. In essence, conservationism was a "Give unto Caesar what is Caesar's, and unto God what is God's" approach to the environment. A specified part of America was protected from developers. The rest of the country was more or less fair game.

Outside government-protected parks and conservancy lands, the only other major impediments to environmental predation in this country during the early decades of the 20th century were local zoning laws. These were mostly intended to insulate well-to-do suburban areas from industrial and commercial pollution. (Before the end of World War II, few people living in suburbs were not well-to-do.)

By the late 1930s and early 1940s, the effects of industrial contamination on people who did not live in prosperous suburbs with acre-plus zoning had become too pronounced to be ignored. Many older American cities were almost terminally polluted. Many areas of rural America had been devastated by bad ecological practices. A substantial part of the New Deal's work programs was directed to correcting these abuses.

A typical example of the environmental situation then prevailing in East Coast cities was in Philadelphia. The solid-waste buildup there was so great that local residents dubbed their metropolis "Filthadelphia." The air was so tainted that pilots flying at less than 5,000 feet were bothered by the stench. Atlantic City, a resort community a few miles up the road, came to be known as the "lungs of Philly," because it was where Philadelphians vacationed when they wanted to breathe.

By the 1940s, the waters of the Delaware River running through the city were unbelievably polluted. Legend has it that Liberty ships docking by the Ben Franklin Bridge overnight had to be repainted after they left the harbor.

It took the combined efforts of city, regional and federal agencies, working over a 30-year period at a cost of billions of dollars, to construct treatment plants and a complex regulatory machinery that brought Philadelphia's air and water up to their present, not overly enticing, condition. Similar efforts were required in almost every major American urban area between the years 1935 and 1970.

Government Involvement Grows

The year 1970 was seminal in the history of American environmentalism. In that year large numbers of people proclaimed at "Earth Day" celebrations across the land that environmental quality-of-life considerations deserved a hearing in the American forum on a par with laissez-faire economic development. Much of the credit for this awakening belongs to Rachel Carson, whose 1962 classic, *Silent Spring*, focused the country's attention on the dangers of unbridled economic development in nonprotected areas of the country.

That same year also saw organized environmentalism blossom into a powerful political force. The Clean Air Act, the first major piece of modern federal environmental legislation with nationwide applications, was passed by Congress that year.

This act has been accurately (if uncharitably) characterized as one of the fuzziest pieces of legislation ever enacted in Washington. Nonetheless, it was a vital first step in creating a legislative and regulatory framework within which all key parts of the country's physical environment could be protected. Many of the early efforts of agencies such as the Environmental Protection Agency (EPA) also fit into this "learn-by-doing" category.

Since 1970, federal environmental legislation has not just been massively expanded in scope and content, it has become a far more refined instrument for establishing parameters of permitted business activities. The Clean Air Act of 1977, for example, was infinitely more sophisticated than the 1970 measure. The clean air proposals being considered by Congress and the Administration in 1989 represent another quantum leap forward in terms of accommodating environmental needs to technical and political realities.

The extraordinarily diverse components of federal environmental policies are now enforced not only by the EPA but also by virtually every federal agency—from the Department of Transportation to the Department of Defense, from the Department of the Interior to the Department of Energy, from the Labor Department to the Department of Agriculture.

During the apple scares of early 1989, the federal Food and Drug Administration (FDA) was in the environmental spotlight because it issues pesticide approvals. Even the Internal Revenue Service gets into the environmental act from time to time. The IRS recently ruled that pollution penalties are not a legitimate business deduction.

As noted in chapter 1, money to enforce all federal legislative and regulatory mandates now on the books has not always been appropriated or spent. Various federal agencies with important environmental responsibilities are thus seriously understaffed. The government has also shown a distinct reluctance to regulate the nation's biggest polluter—itself.

One measure of this failure of self-regulation is the huge radioactive discharges from government nuclear-weapons facilities. The U.S. Department of Energy now estimates that from one facility alone, the Feed Materials Production Center near Fernald, Ohio, more than 297,000 pounds of uranium waste and almost 18,000 pounds of thorium waste were released between 1951 and 1988.

Scores of military bases contain "pink water" sites, bodies of water heavily contaminated with explosive chemicals. Hundreds of federal buildings are in violation of various environmental regulations. Even an EPA headquarters was recently cited for showing symptoms of "sick-building syndrome."

When it comes to leaning on private polluters, however, especially since the waning days of the Reagan Administration, federal laws and regulations are now a for midable instrument for controlling the operation of the private sector. By early 1989, the federal government had obtained pleas or convictions in more than 300 cases involving criminal environmental infractions. Some 231 of these were against individuals, not companies; collec tively, these people were fined more than $13 million.

State and Local Governments Step in

Federal environmental efforts are being strongly supplemented by the activities of state and local enforcers. Today, every state in the Union has a functioning environmental bureaucracy that both implements federal policies and supplements these with its own.

This bureaucratic apparatus has grown to impressive dimensions. The EPA employs more than 16,000 people, including part-timers and occasional consultants. By 1988, according to a resource guide put out by the Center for the Environment and Natural Resources, there were almost 27,000 state environmental bureaucrats, with the largest numbers employed by Pennsylvania, New Jersey and Wisconsin.

California had the largest environmental expenditures of any state, with a 1987 budget exceeding $1 billion. Wyoming allocated the largest percentage of its state budget to the environment—more than 15 percent.

In fields like solid-waste management, states around the country are also moving to take over responsibilities that formerly belonged to their cities and towns. This is not surprising in an era when trash handling often involves carting wastes hundreds and even thousands of miles.

In applying the environmental factor, readers of this book need not become experts in all facets of environmental regulation. Indeed, just keeping environmental professionals up to date on changes in this field has evolved into a thriving industry in its own right. There are scores of newsletters, hundreds of seminars and conferences each year, thousands of in-house specialists and, perhaps, an equal number of consultants working full-time to keep American business "in compliance."

What is important to readers before they apply the environmental factor to personal investing, buying and career decisions, is to have at least an appreciation of just how regulated the general economy has become when it comes to the environment. With that in mind, a brief survey of some of the components of the Great American Environmental Regulation Machine follows.

The Laws

Perhaps the best-known federal environmental laws, other than the Clean Air Act of 1970, are the Safe Drinking Water Act of 1974 (SDWA), which sets national standards for drinking water quality; the Resources Conservation and Recovery Act of 1976 (RCRA), which establishes "cradle-to-grave" procedures for handling newly generated hazardous wastes; and the Comprehensive Environmental Response, Compensation, and Liability Act of 1980 (CERCLA), also known as the "Superfund Act," which outlines government policies with respect to previously generated hazardous waste, identifying and punishing polluters and cleaning up hazardous waste sites.

These measures have been considerably updated and amended since their original passage. CERCLA, for example, was clarified and broadened by the Hazardous and Solid Waste Amendments of 1984 (HSWA). RCRA has been significantly changed and broadened several times since its enactment more than a decade ago. The Clean Air Act was amended in 1977, the Safe Drinking Water Act in 1986.

To this list may be added other relatively well-known and wide-reaching laws: the National Environmental Policy Act of 1970 (NEPA), which requires detailed environmental impact studies on all projects to which the federal government is a party; the Toxic Substances Control Act (TSCA); the Asbestos Hazard Emergency Response Act (AHERA); the Nuclear Waste Policy Act; and the Low-Level Waste Policy Act. Other federal acts relate to ocean dumping and pollution of inland nondrinking-water resources; there are acts aimed at protecting wildlife on land and in coastal waters.

The Federal Insecticide, Fungicide, and Rodenticide Act of 1972 (FIFRA), as amended in 1974 and 1988, has enormous potential to determine how food is produced in this country. Among its provisions are measures that levy fees on pesticide makers, with collected money paying to test their products for environmental safety.

Many key federal laws that were not originally designed to protect the environment now have important environmental provisions. The Occupational Safety and Health Act of 1970, for example, deals mostly with such workplace hazards as faulty wiring and badly maintained stairs. But as amended in 1983 with a Hazard Communication Standard, it has enormous effects on the way companies deal with workplace environmental hazards. The Motor Carrier Act is largely aimed at regulating the trucking industry. It, too, now has "environmental restoration requirements."

Every federal law is interpreted and elaborated into regulations by a government bureaucracy. Failure to comply with these regulations may subject individual and corporate violators to fines, penalties and, on occasion, jail sentences. Thousands of fines, some in the hundred-million-dollar-plus range, were levied on polluters in 1988 by government agencies.

It would be impossible in a space much smaller than several library shelves to note all the environmental regulations and interpretations now on the books of various federal agencies. Noting just a few, however, gives a "flavor" of what regulation in this field means from the economic perspective.

In early 1989, as part of its continuing elaboration of the Occupational Safety and Health Act, the government tightened standards on 212 workplace substances and added 164 new substances to its control list. An estimated cost to industry of these changes is $788 million annually

New EPA rules on handling wastes in ways that protect drinking water from groundwater contamination are expected to cost the average American family $100 a year in higher municipal taxes and fees. Farmers and many small businesses are expected to take an even harder financial hit from these same changes.

Proposed EPA regulations dealing with handling the 8 million tons of sludge dumped annually into U.S. coastal waters may become mandatory by 1991. They could cost municipalities $157 million a year in added treatment expenses. Repairs suggested by government officials for hundreds of thousands of homes with radon contamination could cost property owners between $500 and $2,000 for each site affected.

EPA rulings relating to compliance with a single piece of environmental legislation—the RCRA—now number more than 17,000. When this act is fully implemented in the mid-1990s, corporate compliance with RCRA might cost more than $20 billion annually. Just getting RCRA approval to operate a business today sometimes takes as long as four years and costs as much as a million dollars.

Decisions of the federal bureaucracy have an especially important economic influence on the environmental services industry—for better or worse. An announcement in the fall of 1988 that special liners would be required in landfills to protect groundwater gave a boost to that segment of the industry active in water monitoring. An announcement in late January 1989 that the EPA would use more in-house staff to monitor and correct problems at Superfund sites hurt another segment of the industry—the part that depends on EPA contract work.

To the vast, increasingly pervasive effects of federal environmental regulation on individuals and businesses in all parts of the country must be added the often more immediate consequences of stringent state and municipal environmental rules. Some 2,000 bills or ballot propositions related to toxic-waste handling and recycling were introduced in state legislatures or passed by voters during 1988 alone. The most famous, perhaps, is California's "Proposition 65," a toxic-waste control package so comprehensive it could literally change the way a goodly share of businesses operate in one of the world's largest marketplaces.

New Jersey is a state with exceptionally strong environmental enforcement. Such enforcement is necessary because it is the most densely populated state in the Union, produces the most trash per household (20 pounds per week on average), has the largest number of identified toxic-waste sites and suffers thousands of chemical and oil spills annually.

As is true in 24 other states today, there are laws in New Jersey that dictate whether industrial property is environmentally fit to be sold. State officials have imposed some of the largest fines ever levied against polluters in attempts to reduce dumping. The state administers a comprehensive hazardous-waste cleanup fund, consisting of money from companies operating within New Jersey. Its

Mandatory Source Separation and Recycling Act is among the most far-reaching recycling statutes in the nation. "Environmental Protection" was the seventh largest item in the New Jersey budget in 1989, just behind "Debt Service."

Massachusetts is another long-industrialized state with increasingly active environmental policies—presidential campaign charges about Governor Dukakis's failure to clean up Boston Harbor notwithstanding. To help improve its air, the state's Department of Environmental Quality has announced a temporary moratorium on waste-to-energy incineration.

Along with Vermont, New York, Connecticut, New Jersey, Rhode Island, New Hampshire and Maine, Massachusetts has also instituted new rules requiring gasoline companies to reformulate their products in ways that make them less harmful to the ozone layer.

State laws designed to reduce smog by cutting gasoline emissions have forced service station operators to install new pump nozzles that cut back on emissions. Higher octane requirements, which several northeastern states have imposed on refineries to cut air pollution, have led refinery owners to install their own new equipment. Such attempts by states to solve environmental problems illustrate how local environmental legislation contributes to local inflation.

Pennsylvania is "downriver" from the great chemical works of New Jersey and "downwind" from Ohio and Illinois, where big utilities spew out a goodly share of the ingredients that end up as acid rain. Oil has been pumped in Pennsylvania since the late 1840s. Large-scale coal mining and heavy manufacturing have been major factors in the Pennsylvania economy for many years.

The state's aggressive environmental policies, a response to its profound pollution ills, are therefore not surprising. In a speech in September 1987, Governor Casey compared Pennsylvania's current environmental crisis to the political crisis that faced this country's founders in 1787.

A slew of new environmental legislation has been proposed or passed in Pennsylvania during the last two years. This includes economically significant laws concerning mandatory recycling and a measure that allows liens on the assets of companies with environmental cleanup obligations.

Pennsylvania is now one of four states with their own toxic-waste programs supplementing Superfund. Environmental Resources is the fourth largest department in Pennsylvania's bureaucracy in terms of funding, trailing only Transportation, Public Welfare and Education.

A bit farther north, New York State has another strong mix of environmentally active policies. The solid-waste handling rules recently issued by the state's environmental agency will, by some estimates, boost trash-handling costs 30 percent in the next few years, and are expected to become a model for similar state legislation around the country.

Regional and interregional state environmental cooperation is an increasingly visible element of the national political landscape. In June 1988, the governor of New York joined with the governor of Ohio to ask Congress for stiffer controls over coal-burning plants that produce so much of the acid rain that falls in both states.

On the East Coast, one sees examples of regional cooperation in the activities of the Delaware Basin Water Commission, whose work to protect natural systems has affected business in one of America's most industrialized and populous areas for decades. Across the country, the recent decision of the South Coast Air Quality Management District and the Southern California Association of Governments to bring the Greater Los Angeles area into compliance with national smog standards bodes massive economic change for that area.

Most states in the Northeast now cooperate in disposing of their solid wastes. Waste-to-energy plants are springing up throughout the region. Connecticut currently burns trash "imports" from its neighbors, along with 60 percent of its own garbage. The environmental activities of some other states are worth citing because they hint at ways in which local actions rearrange local economies. Florida, for example, has instituted new rules concerning its 83,000 underground petrochemical tanks—an estimated 15 percent to 20 percent of which are leaking. It also has some of the most stringent laws in the nation governing disposal of lead-acid batteries, motor oil and old tires.

Oklahoma is now collecting a $1.00 fee on new tires to pay for future recycling of old rubber. Michigan allows its taxpayers to deduct money donated to wildlife preservation from their state taxes. The state also has an active program to compost 12 percent of yard wastes by 1993. After the Valdez oil spill, Alaska raised taxes on local petroleum operators.

City governments are another increasingly important source of economically significant environmental regulation. After lack of adequate sewerage capacity led some large California cities like Los Angeles to speak of limiting new residential permits, resale prices for existing homes got a sharp boost in the summer of 1988.

Some idea of other municipal trends on the environmental front may be seen in Minneapolis, Minnesota, and Madison, Wisconsin. In early 1989, the Minneapolis City Council passed the toughest law in the nation to limit plastic packaging. It is expected to have important consequences for the city's retail community when fully implemented in 1990.

Madison's innovative METROGRO program is aimed at turning city sludge into agricultural nutrients. While innovative, METROGRO is far from unique. Indeed, one would be hard-pressed to find a city government of any size anywhere in the United States that is not already active in sludge recycling, leaf recycling or trash recycling. Cities not already conducting recycling programs are letting out contracts to people who will advise the city about how to operate such programs in the future.

New York is a prime example of how various environmental changes are shaping a major urban economy—both for better and for worse. When the city, which produces 25,000,000 tons of trash annually, tried to double its "tipping fee" (collecting fee) for solid waste in the fall of 1988, an industry group, fearing the economic effects of such hikes on its members, successfully sued to have them revoked.

When the city imposed its own set of asbestos removal and handling standards on residential structures as well as school buildings, homeowners discovered it might cost them $700 on average to encapsulate intact asbestos and several thousand dollars to remove the stuff when replacing an old boiler. They also learned that fines for illegally dumping asbestos can run as high as $25,000.

New York City's attempt to set up a ticketing system that will penalize city merchants who fail to control solid-waste buildup on their own doorsteps illustrates how another environmental liability is being converted into a municipal fiscal asset—at the public's expense. Like the city's parking-ticket system, this plan will be highly dependent for success on private companies with city contracts working to make the program a prime revenue-enhancer as well as a trash-reducer.

New York City's solid waste is thus converted into higher indirect taxes. It is also converted into inflation, because more "trash tickets" mean a greater overall cost of

doing business in the city and higher costs of goods as local merchants pass the expense on to their customers.

The Consequences of Regulation

Federal, regional, state and local efforts pertaining to environmental cleanup constitute an overlapping, sometimes contradictory, often politically skewed and
generally inefficient patchwork.

Because governments often cannot pay for their own
environmental laws and regulations, programs with high-
sounding objectives are announced and never enforced.
Because every government is now desperately trying to
pass on environmental costs to other governments (as well
as to business and the general public), courts are more
and more frequently called on to decide who pays for what
environmental cleanup activity and when.

States sue the federal government to act on its own
clean air laws. Cities sue states for funds to run asbestos
removal and handling and recycling programs. Cities and
states countersue each other over where to build low-level
radioactive-waste sites.

Many programs operated by one government do not
solve environmental problems at all—they simply move
the problem into another jurisdiction. Some attempts by
New York and Pennsylvania to dispose of solid waste
added to the solid-waste burden of Ohio. When New York
and New Jersey seek to save their shorelines from sludge
dumping, the sludge as often as not ends up in a Pennsylvania landfill. Ohio industry is saved from costly legislation to prevent acid rain at the cost of higher destructive
ozone levels in central Pennsylvania.

Agencies within the same government administration
frequently work at cross-purposes when it comes to the
environment. The EPA recommends that cars get 40 miles

per gallon to cut air pollution at the same time that the Department of Transportation relaxes requirements that cars get more miles per gallon as a sop to auto manufacturers.

Even different departments within the same agency occasionally run at cross-purposes. Some people at the EPA are now recommending greater use of "nonpolluting" nuclear power plants to check the greenhouse effect, while other people in the same agency are grappling with the difficulties of how to dispose of wastes from existing nuclear plants.

Not surprisingly, confusion and dissention in this realm is downplayed by people in power. Elected officials and government bureaucrats prefer to point to environmental progress made in recent decades, rather than to problems still to be solved or not yet addressed at all.

Unfortunately, the past environmental progress on which officials like to focus has not produced acceptable air, water and soil quality. These programs were geared to smaller, less concentrated populations, and addressed relatively simple technical problems, such as killing bacteria in water and reducing billowing smoke emissions, rather than today's really difficult problems, such as neutralizing heavy metals in drinking water and disposing of the concentrated toxics in smokestack ash.

Past environmental programs improved things temporarily. To maintain standards even at existing—usually unacceptable—levels, however, will require enormous amounts of repair and refurbishment capital, and the future availability of such capital is now very much in question.

Official claims that the overall American environment is improving thus ring hollow. Facts to the contrary are overwhelming. Perhaps the best that can be said about government environmental efforts in recent decades is that they checked the speed of the decline and eliminated a few of the more obvious and blatant symptoms of a sick national environment.

The failure of official efforts to preserve and protect domestic ecosystems through massive regulation is an important concern. From the perspective of this chapter, however, the matter is largely irrelevant.

As even this brief summary demonstrates, government actions, regardless of their effects on the environment, have become a remarkably pervasive tool in creating an environmentally regulated economy. The next chapter looks at the specifics of how such regulation shapes day-to-day operations of major American industries.

CHAPTER 3

An Environment-Shaped Economy

Population growth and more toxic-producing industries are the underlying causes of our present environmental difficulties. Legislation and regulation are the means by which governments seek to control these difficulties. The question that now comes to mind is how these causes and their would-be cures are shaping the U.S. economy.

One could view the environment-economy relationship from a variety of perspectives. Perhaps the best way to understand it, however, is to note the specific effects environmental decline is having on this country's largest industries.

The enormous dollar toll of our past environmental mistakes quickly emerges from such a survey. So, too, do the enormous economic opportunities involved in making things right.

The first industry that comes to mind when one speaks of environmental exposure is petrochemicals. A goodly share of the 2.4 billion pounds of toxic substances released into the atmosphere in 1988, according to the EPA, was generated by this industry. A goodly share of the total multibillion-dollar environmental liabilities that will one day have to be paid for by corporate America is also to be found on properties owned by companies in this group. If changed accounting rules ever require net worth write-downs that accurately reflect environmental exposure, this is where the biggest hits will come.

In addition to this bookkeeping threat, and the ever-present possibility that a Bhopal-style incident will occur on the mainland of America, the present reality of fines and penalties for spills and emissions pervades the industry. Variations on this theme are headlined in newspapers on a daily basis.

"Tenneco Discovers PCBs Along Pipeline; Cleanup To Cost as Much as $30 Million"; "Shell Faces Cost up to $1 Billion for Toxic Waste"; "Occidental Unit Is Ruled Liable in Waste Cases"; "Texas Eastern Unit Formally Agrees to Toxic Cleanup"; "Rohm & Haas May Face $100 Million Cleanup"; "Ashland Oil Pleads No Contest to Charges in Pittsburgh Fuel Spill"; "U.S. Says DuPont Exceeded Limits for Gasoline Lead." These are just a few publicized examples of leak-and-spill costs that are now part of fixed overheads in the petrochemical field.

The most recent example of a petrochemical incident with potentially huge costs to the company involved was, of course, the Exxon tanker oil spill off Valdez, Alaska, in March 1989. This was not the worst tanker spill in history. That dubious honor belongs to the Amoco *Cadiz*, which sank off the coast of France in 1978. But when all the economic ramifications are settled, the Valdez incident may well prove the most costly for the company involved.

Just a month after it occurred, Exxon had been hit with 31 suits and 1,300 claims—including a $2-billion-plus class action against it and Alaska Pipeline Service Co. Exxon had also begun hiring the 4,000 people it estimated would be needed to clean up 305 miles of Alaskan shoreline at a cost of several hundred million dollars.

Less direct, but possibly longer-lasting, economic fall-out to Exxon from the spill was taking shape as well. Some managers of large pension funds met with the company to express their displeasure with the incident. The company's offices were picketed, and boycotts against its service stations and credit cards were organized. Worst of all was the threat the spill raised to plans for further drilling on the North Slope of Alaska, the nation's richest remaining petroleum reserve, and a place where Exxon is part of a group seeking expanded exploration rights.

Not all the costs of a Valdez-like spill are paid by petrochemical companies themselves, of course. Many are picked up by insurers. Each spill and leak does work to raise a petrochemical firm's insurance premiums, however, and fines and penalties assessed by government are usually not covered by insurance.

Another thing not covered by insurance is the capital costs associated with changed or tightened compliance standards that are inevitable by-products of well-publicized accidents. New anti-smog legislation recently introduced in the Los Angeles area, for example, will require the Chevron Corporation to spend as much as $180 million on emission-reducing equipment at one of its refineries there.

On an even wider scale, DuPont in 1988 spent an estimated $600 million to operate and maintain solid waste disposal, air and water pollution control programs and set aside another $220 million that year to meet future remediation commitments. Monsanto spent approximately $207 million in 1988 to operate and maintain its own environmental program.

While being keenly aware of investment risks that environmental exposure represents for petrochemical firms, one must also be alert to nuances when applying the environmental factor The black-or-white approach often favored by environmental groups does not always play well here.

Just as the AIDS epidemic is receding in the homosexual community because gays were the first to feel the full force and fury of that disease, and were therefore the first to adopt practices that help slow its spread, petrochemical companies were the first major sector of the economy to feel the full force of environmental regulation. The response of many companies has been to get on the environmental cleanup bandwagon.

DuPont, for example, not only began phasing out production of ozone-harming chlorofluorocarbons (CFCs) in early 1988 but it has become a leader in formulating and patenting replacement compounds. Others in the crowded field of large and small corporations seeking CFC replacements include AT&T, which announced plans to market a CFC substitute that can be used in circuit board manufacture.

DuPont is also moving to become a leader in the fast-developing plastic recycling business. Working with Waste Management, Inc., it plans to establish the largest plastic recycling operation in the country, which will handle some 40 million pounds of plastic containers annually in years to come. A Mobil Oil affiliate is also active in plastic recycling. So, too, is Arco Chemical. Dow Chemical will be working with Domtar, Inc., on a program to recycle plastic milk and soft drink containers.

W. R. Grace, which received so much bad environmental press for operations at one of its Massachusetts-based plants some years ago, is moving into the creation of natural pesticides, and bought a 33 percent interest in a leading environmental firm in 1988 (Canonie Environmental Services). Union Carbide has a patented sludge-digesting process. The Atlantic Richfield Company is a petroleum firm hedging its energy bets through ownership of a subsidiary that manufactures photovoltaic solar cells. The

Shell Group runs reforesting programs in at least four countries.

When some environmentalists think of General Electric and Westinghouse Electric, they think of nuclear plant construction. Today, the former is active in a variety of pollution cleanup endeavors, including disposal of nuclear wastes. The latter builds and operates waste-to-energy facilities.

Collectively, in fact, the combined "sideline" activities of petrochemical companies probably represent the biggest single component of the environmental services industry. Looking down the road, one suspects this diversification might prove to be the salvation of many firms—and of the capital of their investors as well.

Down on the Farm

Environmental headlines about agriculture and related food-producing industries in recent months have often focused on climatic changes. The so-called greenhouse effect, brought about by excessive burning of fossil fuels and by other man-made emissions, is thought by many scientists to be altering weather patterns in ways that could seriously hurt output in America's grain belt. The fact that six of the warmest years in this century have occurred in the 1980s is but one indication that greenhouse-effect theories have considerable substance.

Grains are this country's biggest cash export. We sold more than $35 billion worth abroad in 1988 while importing less than $20 billion worth of agricultural products. Any reduction in our ability to produce excess grain to sell abroad would further worsen an already bleak national trade balance situation.

More and more, the key to international competitiveness in agricultural markets is producing "cleaner" (i.e., less contaminated) grains. A disturbing manifestation of how we may be falling behind in this regard involved the 1988 U.S. corn crop. Much of this crop (10 times more than occurs in a normal year) was tainted with aflatoxin, a toxin produced by a naturally occurring fungus, which spreads whenever drought conditions exist and is dangerous to both farm animals and humans in high enough concentrations.

The Midwest warms because of the greenhouse effect. Droughts ensue. Aflatoxin contamination spreads. The value of U.S. grain production falls. This is an increasingly common type of linkage between environmental deterioration and economic deterioration.

Beyond the greenhouse peril, there are other facets of the pollution-agriculture equation with serious economic implications. Some 2.6 billion pounds of chemical pesticides, sold under 50,000 different brand names and together generating $20 billion a year in sales for their producers, are sprayed on crops by American farmers each year.

One economic offshoot of this practice is the rising costs of treating thousands of agricultural workers who are exposed to these often-toxic chemicals. A study published in the *American Journal of Public Health*, which stated that women residing in counties where pesticides are widely used have twice the risk of having a child with birth defects as women living elsewhere, hints at one price paid by nonagricultural members of our population for excessive pesticide use.

More such hints are turning up with alarming frequency. The EPA has reported pesticides in the groundwater of 38 states—notably the pesticide aldicarb, which has also shown up in potatoes and bananas. A report from the National Resources Defense Council cited traces of pesticide residues on many fruits and vegetables in supermarkets around the country. In a separate report, the U.S.

Public Interest Research Group said that 25 chemicals with possible carcinogenic properties were commonly used in raising corn, 23 in tomatoes and 21 in peaches.

That all-time American favorite fruit, the apple, became the subject of an intense pollution debate in early 1989. Dozens of school systems around the country stopped selling and serving apples and apple juice in their cafeterias because of health fears. The apple industry moved to counter these actions by running its own ad campaign.

In 1972 fears about DDT spraying of produce caused that chemical to be outlawed. Since then, there have been similar health scares about lead arsenate in grapefruit and pesticide traces in watermelons. For decades, in fact, the increase in the number of chemicals used to make produce last longer and look better has greatly outstripped the government's capacity to monitor their health effects on humans. The economic consequences of the public uneasiness these reports generated are now being felt.

Whether health fears about eating apples and other fruits and vegetables are, in fact, warranted, the changed production methods they are forcing growers to use may soon cost consumers dearly in economic terms. Already, just accommodating the EPA's changing standards for various pesticides and fungicides is beginning to contribute to inflation on the food front.

A buzz term in agricultural circles these days is "integrated pest management." This refers to a technique that uses more natural pest predators and crop rotation and less chemicals in producing crops. From a health perspective, it has much to offer vis-à-vis the present high chemical dosage agriculture. But it also costs more to implement—with the higher costs passed along to food consumers.

When one speaks of agribusiness, one thinks of poultry and livestock, as well as of grains, fruits and vegetables. Since the late 1970s, literally millions of chickens have had to be destroyed because of contamination of feed with pesticides suspected of causing cancer.

Economic threats to livestock producers were also evident in a recent European ban on American cattle fed with certain growth hormones. These hormones cannot themselves be classified as an environmental risk. But the adverse pronouncements about their presence in American beef hints at a growing queasiness among Western European consumers about foodstuffs of any kind that are perceived as tainted.

These same consumers might one day avoid American beef fed with aflatoxin-tainted grains. The Green Movement now spreading in West Germany and elsewhere on the continent is more than just a political expression of environmentalism. It has a very strong personal purification motive, which encourages seeking out and buying natural foods. It is not inconceivable that persons involved in the Green Movement will one day lead boycotts of all environmentally suspect American agricultural products.

Developments in the American timber industry show yet another link between environmental economics and agribusiness. Here, too, pollution is reshaping the way producers do business and their prospects for future profits.

An acid rain map of the United States shows areas of prime contamination along the eastern seaboard from Maine down to Central Florida, patches of serious blight in the Upper Great Lakes region, and other "black belts" in the Pacific Northwest. A study by the World Resources Institute estimates annual overall forest and farmland losses from such pollution to be around $5 billion.

Commercially important timber crops like yellow pine have been especially hard-hit. Specialty crops, like the maple trees that are the basis of a $200-million-a-year maple syrup industry, have been seriously hurt. Facts like these led the American Forestry Association in late 1987 to issue a report saying that "the risks and costs associated with further delaying pollution controls now seem to outweigh the risks and costs associated with action."

The $30 billion a year commercial fishing industry is another casualty of acid rain and other pollutants. A recent EPA report confirms the general conclusion that many of the lakes and streams in the eastern United States have lost much of their ability to support marine life; and a more focused study by the New York Environmental Protection Agency stated that a full quarter of that state's Adirondack Mountains' lakes and ponds were no longer conducive to fish life cycles because of acid rain.

Coastal fishing in the Atlantic Ocean has been seriously affected, not only by acid rain but also by massive sewage and industrial contamination. In spite of the fact that some $70 billion has been spent by governments since 1972 to improve their sewage-treatment systems, more than twice as much sewage is now dumped into waterways feeding the Atlantic Ocean than was dumped in the early 1970s.

Boston, for example, still discharges 500 million gallons of sewage a day into its harbor. The result? One-third of the clam flats around that harbor are closed.

Pollution-linked fish kills in the waters off New Jersey are common. Many fish now caught along the North Carolina coast have mysterious sores, which do little to enhance their marketability. Phosphates and untreated sewage have wreaked havoc with fish catches in Chesapeake Bay. Contamination alerts on fish caught in the Great Lakes have been common since the mid-1970s. The Valdez oil spill is threatening not only aquatic life but also the profits of Alaska's $3-billion-a-year fishing industry.

In addition to the negative effects pollution has had on New Jersey fishermen, the far more serious economic effects on that state's tourist business should also be pointed out. The number of visitors to the Jersey Shore, a popular resort area, dropped 22 percent between the summer of 1987 and the summer of 1988, largely because of beach contamination. Even factoring in higher prices charged by businesses in the area, gross revenues along the Jersey Shore in 1988 were down more than eight percent.

New Jersey's tourist industry is far from being the only such industry hurt by spreading pollution. Sewage closed stretches of beaches in New York in 1988, causing the tourist industry on Long Island to lose an estimated $1.8 billion. Dirty air and fear of high ozone levels are reducing the attraction of once pristine places like Acadia National Park in Maine.

It is difficult to quantify the exact costs to the American tourist industry of environmental deterioration. One suggestion of how great these costs might soon be, however, is to be found in a recent study from the U.S. Fish and Wildlife Service. It found that almost three-quarters of all Americans over 16 are active participants in wildlife-related activities. One corollary of such a finding, of course, is that when such activities are rendered less attractive, tourism will suffer.

Of Transport and Energy

One of the major revolutions in automaking and marketing during the 1970s involved "down-sizing" and improvements in fuel efficiency. These changes were brought about by oil price rises and fears of petroleum shortages.

These fears have since moderated. Cars are again getting bigger and people are driving more. As the challenges of an ever-more-polluted environment grow, however, it is not hard to imagine a time in the very near future when automakers, and indeed all sectors of the transportation industry, will have to bow to environmental imperatives as they once did to OPEC dictates.

There are now some 400 million vehicles operating around the world. Together, they contribute mightily to airborne pollution. A publication of the Worldwatch Institute in Washington, D.C., estimates these vehicles emit some 547 million tons of carbon into the atmosphere annually. Officials at the National Precipitation Assessment Program estimate that the bulk of this country's 20 million tons of nitrogen oxides in the air come from auto emissions.

In spite of much improved efficiency standards that have boosted average fuel consumption of cars in this country from 13 to 18 miles a gallon since 1973, the possibility that limitations on private travel will become commonplace is again growing. During summer 1988's heat wave and serious air inversions, New Jersey was on the verge of declaring a travel emergency that would have kept private cars out of some urban areas.

Some states (e.g., Ohio) have been threatened with cutoffs of their federal highway funds for failing to have auto emission inspection programs. Cities—Denver among them—are toying with plans to limit truck traffic at certain hours to help alleviate local smog problems.

In March 1989, the Southern California Association of Governments, which includes representatives from Los Angeles County, voted to approve a 123-point air-cleanup plan aimed at bringing the smog-ridden region into compliance with federal standards on all air pollutants by early in the next century. The plan requires 40 percent of the area's cars and 70 percent of its trucks to operate on "alternative" fuels by the year 2007. The clean air proposals made by President Bush in June 1989 called for auto makers to reduce tail pipe emissions by 40 percent in five years.

These foreshadow things to come. Whether auto and truck manufacturers retool to meet far tougher emission standards demanded by far worse air quality, whether they move more rapidly into ethanol-powered vehicles or electric cars, whether they diversify into production of mass-transit rather than private vehicles, the consequences of environmental deterioration for the transportation sector will be great.

The question of which materials meet tomorrow's environmental standards is yet another problem facing vehicle manufacturers. The bankruptcy of one of this country's largest makers of asbestos clutch and brake parts illustrates such growing business hazards.

Car and truck manufacturers appreciate all these risks. Developing contingency plans aimed at reducing emissions while improving fuel economy and using the least environmentally destructive materials possible are among their most pressing engineering priorities.

Environmental challenges are even greater for another pillar of the American economic system—utilities. The utility industry's ongoing nuclear crisis is equivalent to Detroit's energy crisis in the 1970s and early 1980s. This nuclear crisis is far from being settled and is fast merging with the larger question of how to cope with extra electricity demands associated with sweltering summers on a planet heated by the greenhouse effect.

Just as there is no effective program in place to handle this country's nuclear weapons-related wastes (and precious little agreement about how one might be organized and funded), there is a wealth of confusion about how to handle past, present and future civilian-generated nuclear waste materials. The low-level variety is supposed to be rendered harmless in state-operated facilities. Not surprisingly, this democratic disposal approach has raised hackles among local people wherever a low-level site has been proposed.

Finding a permanent resting place for the more dangerous nuclear wastes is a problem that has defied solution for three decades. At the time of this writing, federal officials are desperately trying to get a long-range storage facility for spent commercial nuclear fuel approved in Yucca Mountain near the old Nevada nuclear test range.

Energy Department officials have even floated an idea to let private contractors set up their own handling sites for moderate-level wastes. Whether *any* permanent nuclear disposal plan is practical for highly and moderately radioactive wastes, given the extensive length of time this material is a threat to human health, is a question frequently raised by independent critics.

Achieving a solution to problems linked to nuclear waste of any kind seems fraught with enormous difficulties these days. In February 1989, for example, the federal Atomic Safety and Licensing Board gave permission for the operator of the Three Mile Island nuclear facility to evaporate 2.3 million gallons of water that was tainted during the accident at that plant in March 1979.

It took ten years to reach consensus regarding this material, which is very far from being the most reactive of wastes. Even so, implementation of the decision was still being delayed, pending appeals.

Ongoing problems of disposal, actual accidents like the one at Three Mile Island in Pennsylvania, the biggest municipal bond default in history involving bonds for two nuclear units owned by the Washington Public Power Supply System, huge losses reported by nuclear-operating utilities from Texas to Long Island, a distaste for nuclear plants generally by a majority of Americans—all have worked to make nuclear-generated power a bad economic investment for utilities during the past decade.

Increased fear of nuclear pollution in the wake of Chernobyl simply accentuated this feeling. In the United States today, it takes an average of 13 years to get a license approved to operate a nuclear power plant.

While nuclear pollution fears and their related costs are growing, so are fears associated with coal-burning power plants. These plants are prime contributors to acid rain pollution. In fact, about two-thirds of the sulfur dioxide component of acid rain and one-third of its nitrogen oxide components are spewed out by electric utilities that have not installed expensive scrubber equipment.

A 1978 Brookhaven National Laboratory study estimated that the health of almost 37,000 people a year is impaired by pollution from coal-fired plants. The acid rain generated by coal burning has become a major bone of contention with Canada, the recipient of much of this pollutant. One of the first acts of newly elected President Bush was to call for a 274 percent increase in spending on cleaner coal-burning technologies.

At the time of this writing, it appears Congress and the Administration are getting ready to pass another, more stringent version of the Clean Air Act. No matter what its final form, some new environmental burdens will certainly end up being put on America's power-producing industry. If passed as outlined by the President in June 1989, costs to electric power users in some midwestern states could also rise 15 percent.

Insurance and Banking

Superficially, the level of environmental exposure seems less great for another pillar of the American economy: the insurance industry. On closer examination, however, the economic dangers to insurers, dangers related to environmental decline, turn out to be enormous.

An important legal decision in 1984 established the principle of "strict retroactive liability" with respect to the environment. This means, in essence, that businesses are responsible for environmental cleanup costs on the properties they currently own, even if the pollution was not deliberate, even if it was not a crime at the time it occurred, and even if a past owner of the property did the polluting. After this decision, the insurance industry hastened to get out of the pollution liability coverage business, except for a few specialty insurers offering policies featuring very tight underwriting. Consequently, "pollution insurance" covering incremental, nonaccidental environmental damages is hard to come by and extremely expensive. As in other arenas dominated by tort law, where settlements can be staggering and adequate actuarial histories on which to base appropriate premium rates are lacking, insurers have, by-and-large, opted to confront this facet of the "liability crisis" by exiting the field as expeditiously as possible.

Unfortunately for them, this has not always proved easy. The line between "sudden" environmental damages of the kind still covered by business accident policies and "gradual" damages no longer covered can be quite fine. Courts are now hearing cases in which companies charged with polluting are claiming that their present or pre-1984 insurance covers all or part of their pollution liabilities.

More than 100 such cases, at least one of which involves more than a billion dollars, are being heard at the time of this writing. In one litigation, a single corporation is suing 270 different insurers to cover its environmental obligations.

If judges and juries rule a certain way in these cases, the negative effects on the balance sheets of some insurers could be enormous. Just how enormous was evident in remarks made by the chief executive officer of a leading casualty insurance firm before a recent meeting of the National Press Club. Speaking about what might happen if insurers were allocated too large a share of the environmental burden, he noted that "the estimated costs necessary to correct environmental damage (in this country) exceed the total surplus of the entire U.S. insurance industry."

While incremental, cumulative environmental damages may or may not end up being charged to insurance firms, there seems little likelihood that these firms can avoid charges for environment damage of the accidental variety. When Ashland Oil made good on its huge 1988 oil spill in Pittsburgh, its insurer did the paying. The biggest part of Union Carbide's $470-million Bhopal settlement was borne by insurance companies. When all the courtroom smoke has cleared on Exxon's Valdez spill, insurers will doubtless have felt the pinch.

There are many other emerging pitfalls for certain sectors of the insurance industry, both in the growing environmental crisis and in government attempts to check its growth. One typical example: When Massachusetts tried to enforce its own Superfund-like legislation in 1987 (a law that seemed to burden property owners with greater environmental liability), three title insurance firms in the state threatened to stop writing policies.

Along with pitfalls, however, environmental problems are also creating some lucrative new opportunities for insurers. At least one company that has long been active in repairing leaking underground tanks in Florida, for example, is now in the process of setting up a specialty insurance subsidiary that will supply firms (mostly in the petrochemical business) with leak insurance.

Asbestos contamination of buildings, which may cost $100 billion to repair in the next decade, is another "opportunity" for insurers. A fair number are currently in the process of offering coverage for asbestos cleanup costs to building owners.

In looking at the insurance industry and the environment, it is important to keep in mind how many other industries are affected by an inability to get environmental coverage. Inability to get insurance has long plagued environmental services firms and kept many contractors from asbestos and hazardous-waste work. It will almost certainly be an indirect cause of thousands of bankruptcies in scores of other industries in years to come.

Some of the same environmental worries causing nervousness among insurers are at work in the allied banking business. It was not until relatively recently that lenders started getting attuned to potential losses related to pollution. Now, it is one of the hottest topics of conversation among leaders in lending circles.

There are few banks, for example, that will now provide commercial mortgage money without an environmental audit of a property. On a larger scale, when ownership of some bankrupt Texas thrifts was transferred to new owners by the Federal Bank Board in early 1989, the board had to promise to indemnify the new owners for future toxic-waste–related costs if these were discovered within a specified period.

The increased environmental exposure of lenders making certain types of business loans is another growing source of concern for banks. In Boston, the State Street Bank has been sued by companies claiming that it became a "co-operator" of a toxic site when it tried to recover a loan made to a firm hired to clean that site.

Moving higher up the banking ladder, the lending buzzword at the World Bank in the last year or two has been modified from "growth" to "sustainable growth." Once upon a time, this institution's primary interest was to foster industrialization and resource exploitation at whatever environmental cost. Now, its directors have come to see that this is a prescription for an economic turnaround that will hurt, rather than help, a developing nation's future ability to service debt.

Other international lenders are reaching the same conclusion. The Inter-American Development Bank and the Agency for International Development have both begun to shift their policies in ways that preserve the ability of natural systems to keep producing year after year.

It might also be borne in mind that the world's biggest lender is the U.S. government, with a $250-billion loan portfolio of its own, and legal obligations to back more than $450 billion in private loans. If too many of these go belly up because of environmental decline, the spinoffs for American taxpayers could be most unpleasant.

Economy-Wide Concerns

As the above survey demonstrates, the list of industries whose operations are already reeling under the weight of environmental pressures is impressive. And as one thinks the matter through and does a bit of research, it becomes clear that hardly any major component of the U.S. economy could be excluded from such a list.

Steel-making? The biggest single fine levied when the EPA tagged 25 firms for failing to report emissions of dangerous toxics recently was levied on a steel company with a plant in Indiana.

Computers? Xerox recently agreed to pay more than $4 million to families in settlement of a suit involving a chemical leak. On the software side, according to a trade magazine, more than 400 programs that tell governments and companies what they need to know about environmental compliance are now on the market—double the number available just a year earlier.

Recreation? One of the largest amusement parks in the world was cited and fined in late 1988 for failing to handle its hazardous wastes properly. In a Universal City, California, amusement park, a new ride simulates an earthquake, with all its attendant environmental implications.

Building supplies? The $2.5-billion trust fund the Mansville Corporation was obligated to establish to pay asbestos claimants suggests potential liabilities for companies in this business. Even at the retail level, sellers of building supplies must now take greater care in the products they handle.

Aerospace? Landsat satellites are among the most important tools for tracking both domestic and worldwide environmental decline. As a growth market for rocket hardware and associated technology, environmental "eyes in the sky" have enormous potential.

Packaging? With a third of this country's solid wastes now consisting of wrapping materials and containers, dramatic changes in this field are underway. For example, sales of resins that go into plastic packages, a $28-billion market in 1988, could fall off in years to come if solid-waste disposal costs continue to escalate.

There are environmental health issues related to packaging, too. Not long ago Greenpeace petitioned the Depart ment of Agriculture to require changed packaging for the 5 billion milk containers used in school lunch programs, citing a dioxin risk in containers made from bleached paper. This move might also bode ill for the 150 pulp and paper mills in North America that make this packaging material.

Biotech? While fears of environmental contamination are slowing or stopping scores of biotech companies from developing hoped-for products, other firms in the field are finding exciting new opportunities in the fight to clean up pollution. The story here can be neatly summed up in a headline that appeared not so long ago in a leading business publication: " 'Super' Microbes Offer Way to Treat Hazardous Waste." The cost of biological remediation as a way to render toxic wastes harmless is estimated to be just one percent of chemical treatment methods.

Mining? If a mining company operates on more than five acres of land, it is required to post a bond with the government to ensure that the land will be restored to something like its original state once mining operations are completed. The ultimate profitability of many strip mining companies is thus closely linked to how much they end up paying to restore local environments that their operations temporarily disrupt.

The ability of gold mines to stay open is now highly dependent on how well they manage the cyanide compounds they use in their operations. The profits of uranium mines hinge on demand for a fuel whose use has been seriously affected by environmental protest. Profits of asbestos mine operators certainly did not boom in the wake of the Mansville bankruptcy.

Coal mining has a very high environmental sensitivity. The industry as a whole has been in a steady decline for decades. In a state such as Pennsylvania, for example, where 108,000 people made their living mining coal at the start of this century, just 17,000 miners are employed today. New clean air legislation aimed at acid-rain emissions could cripple the domestic coal industry still further.

The legal profession? By mid-1988 there were 5,000 attorneys specializing in environmental matters. Most practiced in states with strict environmental laws, such as California and New Jersey. The overwhelming majority were not would-be worldsavers, sporting earth shoes and Fu Manchu moustaches a la 1970s stereotypes, but defenders of status quo corporations against environmental challenges from government and suits by other corporations.

The size of recent legal settlements in this field and the increasing complexity of applicable rules and regulations virtually assure a steep increase in the number of environmental lawyers in years to come. Given the many confusing environmental laws that now apply to land-use and real estate, no sensible developer even considers a project today without first going through its environmental implications with an attorney.

Beyond servicing corporations, attorneys are finding other opportunities involving the environment. The overriding desire of all Americans to lay the environmental burden on someone else, combined with the litigious nature of our society, guarantees that lawyers will do well in this realm in years to come. By some estimates, an astounding 30 percent to 60 percent of all money spent since 1980 on "the environment" has actually gone into legal fees.

One could jump from industry to industry, looking at all the components that make up the U.S. economy, and be hard-pressed to find more than a handful that are not feeling the effects of environmental deterioration—or of laws and regulations meant to check its spread. Whether an environment-shaped economy is a good thing or not is, therefore, no longer worth debating.

Just as one no longer need love nature to see the necessity of practicing sound environmental life-styles, one need not approve of the way the economy is being skewed to protect the physical environment to adapt personal economic and business approaches to accommodate this fact.

The world is a certain way. Sensible people make the necessary adjustments. On the matter of the environment, past excesses now shape, to an unprecedented degree, present and future economic choices.

PART II

The Environmental Factor and Investing

CHAPTER 4

The Environmental Factor and Health Care

When speaking of environmental deterioration and various industries, two exceptionally important parts of the economy come to mind: health care and real estate.

This chapter explores health-care issues and environmental problems because of the extraordinarily prominent role health care plays in the overall economy. Chapter 5 is devoted to real estate because it is the basis of middle-class wealth in this country and because so many elements of pollution now affect property values.

The sheer size of health programs and services in the United States is awesome. More than 11 percent of this country's gross national product went into health spending in 1988—$558.7 billion in all. The corporate liability for health-care costs of retired employees alone is estimated to exceed $400 billion.

If one wants to toss numbers around, it is easy to find many that hint at how great health-care costs stemming from various forms of environmental pollution are to society. The American Lung Association, for example, estimates that more than $40 billion a year must be spent caring for people with ills related to air pollution.

The same organization estimates that 62 percent of the U.S. population in 487 counties now breathes air that does not meet public health standards. In recent congressional testimony, an association spokesperson suggested that as many as 60 percent of this country's children and old people may suffer some form of respiratory problem as a result.

The danger for children is reminiscent of the air pollution situation in Mexico City (cited earlier in this book) that caused schools to be closed for a month so that students could have a "breathing spell." A doctor with the American Academy of Pediatrics, commenting on high ozone levels recorded in many U.S. cities during 1988, suggested that it might now be "prudent" to limit children's play in these areas to prevent acute respiratory problems.

In June 1989, a preliminary report from the EPA suggested that people living near 205 high polluting industrial sites around the country had far greater risks of contracting cancer than other Americans.

If one wishes to demonstrate a relationship between environmental decline and declining public health with anecdotes, the pages of medical journals and daily newspapers are filled with stories linking pollution to sickness. One typical report hints that Alzheimer's disease is caused by aluminum contamination of drinking water. Another speaks of links between cancer and a chemical commonly sprayed on apples to make them look better.

Other headlines cite health risks from lead in water coolers. Low-birth-weight babies and high incidences of leukemia have both been mentioned in stories about old landfills-cum-Superfund sites. CFC damage to the ozone layer is blamed for everything from cataracts to cancers. Towns in West Virginia and Pennsylvania where mining economies once flourished are now populated by people too poor to move who are suffering from exorbitant cancer and miscarriage rates.

If one were to total all the links between environmental deterioration and rising health costs—the connections between tainted air, tainted water, tainted soil and escalating medical bills; the innumerable real and potential relationship of "sick buildings" to the work performance and output of the people who work in them; the increasingly disturbing way just eating contaminated fruits, vegetables, grains and meats is running up the national health bill—the amount of money involved would be so intimidating as to seem incredible. And the data we have in these areas are still only fragmentary and partial.

The comments of a senior scientist with the Environmental Defense Fund sum up just how limited our knowledge is regarding what it could cost to care for people suffering from different forms of environmental health blight. "There are 60,000 chemicals in use, and on 80 percent of them there is absolutely no data," she was quoted as saying. "Generally, we are in the dark about what these chemicals can or cannot do."

In Context

To understand the burden that environment related ills will put on the U.S. economy generally and the U.S. health system in particular, one must understand that these ills are part of a larger "chronic health care crisis." The average American life span was 47 years at the start of this century. It is about 75 years today. The fastest growing segment of the population today consists of people in the eighties. This aging explosion is putting an enormous cost strain on national health resources.

So, too, is the AIDS epidemic. In centuries past, plagues killed people quickly—and cheaply. AIDS sufferers die slowly, and treatment in their final months or years can cost $50,000 or more.

Exploding costs of coping with chronic maladies associated with old age—exploding costs of treating other chronic ills, such as AIDS and various forms of cancer—these form the context in which to view the added, potentially even greater, long-term health-care costs directly or indirectly related to environmental decline.

Few environment-related ills kill quickly or cheaply. Whether they are malignancies caused by an apparently endless number of cancer-causing substances now circulating in our air and water and food or congenital lung problems caused by breathing smog or interior pollutants, most disable gradually and take their toll in pain, discomfort and dollars over a period of many years.

The majority of environmental ills do not even "disable," in the ordinary meaning of that term. Nonetheless, the economic price these maladies levy on society is massive.

We are just beginning to understand the thousands of major and minor extra burdens on our health care systems brought about by tainted air. We are just starting to measure the health costs of heavy metals in drinking water and pesticides on the fruits and vegetables we consume. Agencies like the EPA have been conducting studies on the health risks of smog for a dozen years and still have not reached any definitive conclusions.

Facts on cancers (and the cost of treating them) caused by living too close to old toxic-waste dumps are only starting to trickle in. The economic costs to society of lost productivity from people forced to work in buildings where toxic substances are present or to drive to work through pervasive smog conditions may take decades to gather and analyze.

Even if the environment were in pristine condition, the demographics of aging and the rise of related or parallel long-term-care costs would threaten the future solvency of our already overburdened health-care system. The massive additional economic burdens spawned by a sickened environment make the specter even more frightening.

The Economic Response

One positive aspect of the spread of environment-related health problems is the growing investment, employment and entrepreneurial opportunities opening up for health-care professionals and people in associated disciplines. For better or worse, this has become a major area of economic activity today.

As part of their full-service approach to environmental services, a number of companies that clean up site pollution also have established divisions that check sites for environmental health risks. This activity qualifies both as preventive medicine and as protection against future litigation.

These firms test a workplace for environmental risks and interpret gathered data. They offer corrective engineering when required. They work out preventive programs to eliminate (or at least modify) future environmental health claims.

Drug testing is an important source of income for many smaller laboratories. Frequently, the same equipment that can spot traces of illegal drugs can also be used to analyze samples for dangerous environmental contamination. This overlap is the reason why quite a few laboratories that are looking to expand their marketing bases are seriously considering the potential of environmental testing.

As institutions, hospitals are major polluters. The average American hospital generates 10 to 15 pounds of waste per day per patient. Handling this "red bag" waste has become a large business for many environmental services firms, including the two largest entities in the field, Waste Management, Inc., and Browning-Ferris.

In hospitals themselves, there are a growing number of medical specialists in everything from environmental psychology (treating people who have been exposed to large doses of toxics) to toxicologists who prescribe for the physical symptoms of such exposure. There is now an active and growing American Academy of Environmental Medicine.

Given the excess number of hospital beds in the United States and the need of many institutions to find a field in which to specialize merely to survive, it seems only a matter of time before environmental health centers are established in urban centers around the country.

CHAPTER 5

The Environmental Factor and Real Estate

If one group could be singled out for its sharply increased awareness about how environmental deterioration shapes asset values, it would probably be real estate professionals. Many of these people have learned the hard way that when one owns land or buildings today, one also owns all the environmental hassles that come with each.

A similar awareness is gradually trickling down to the general public. The reasons are obvious. Not only is home ownership the biggest single component of middle-class wealth in the United States but rents from residential properties rank among the most important sources of small business income.

Much of the wealth of companies in which individuals invest directly is based on real property. Much of the wealth in which people invest indirectly, through pension funds and insurance policies, is also real estate-based.

The threat to real estate values in all property sectors—residential, commercial, industrial—from environment-related causes is potentially far greater than threats from higher interest rates, a deep recession or virtually any other cause one might care to name. The relationship between property values and "the health of the land" is thus immediate, intimate, visceral.

Beginning with the Family Home

The best place to begin looking at this relationship is the family home. In recent years a combination of soaring prices and tighter borrowing standards has made home ownership a far harder dream for Americans to realize than it was in decades past. But a majority of families in this country still own rather than rent and still view home equity as their primary (and sometimes their only) source of family savings.

What are the environmental challenges to this asset? In terms of worst-case scenarios, they include the discovery that one's home is on or near an old toxic-waste site. That happened to people in Love Canal, New York, and Times Beach, Missouri.

The Love Canal story is perhaps the best known. For a period of ten years, between 1942 and 1953, more than 21,000 tons of chemical wastes were dumped in this pleasant suburban area near Niagara Falls, New York. By the 1970s the waste had worked its way into the soil, the water and the air of the community.

By 1978 things had deteriorated to the point where New York State was forced to declare a health emergency in the area. Thousands of residents were subsequently evacuated or left voluntarily. Hundreds of houses were bulldozed out of existence. The Love Canal tragedy was the catalyst that led to the establishment of the federal Superfund.

Love Canal is the archetypal homeowner's environmental horror story. But in many less painful incarnations, it is happening to people around the country—people who discover their properties are near one of the 1,100-plus sites that the EPA has placed on its Superfund priority list and targeted for fast cleanup action

Not all of these priority sites are in rural or out-of-the-way areas, either. One of the most notorious is a private home in Lansdowne, a Philadelphia suburb. During the 1930s and 1940s a professor at the University of Pennsylvania set up a laboratory in the basement of this home in which he processed radium that area physicians used in cancer treatments.

Estimated costs of returning this property and surrounding areas to a safe condition have risen steadily and now exceed $9.5 million. The work involves digging down nine feet and removing more than 1,000 tons of contaminated earth, which is then shipped to a low-level radioactive dump facility in Utah.

In worst-case scenarios, affected property owners are generally buffeted by a variety of woes. The most serious, of course, are the health problems that may result from long-time exposure to certain toxics, and the fear of cancer that people exposed to these toxics bear for their entire lives. Children of former Love Canal residents have reportedly been born with two rows of teeth and missing kidneys

Often, there is little or no economic compensation for these ills and the associated fears that go with them. Former Love Canal residents, for example, were paid an average of $35,000 for their properties by the state and received court settlements that were typically in the $5,000 to $15,000 range. Times Beach residents lost a negligence suit filed against chemical companies they blamed for spraying dioxins near their one-time homes. They ended up with nothing in the way of court settlements.

Along with health and economic woes, proximity of one's home to a priority Superfund site can lead to all the troubles and indignities that come in the wake of involuntary relocation. The time, effort and expense of becoming involved in lengthy litigation adds yet another layer of unpleasantness to the experience.

When residential property is not close to a priority cleanup site but is near one of the 28,000 less-contaminated locations identified by the EPA, losses to property owners can range from the miniscule to the disastrous. The same is true about the additional locales now turning up on toxic-site lists generated by state governments.

New Jersey is by many standards the most toxic-ridden state in the Union (though Louisiana is probably a close second). By mid-1988, New Jersey housed 96 Superfund sites—twice as many as runner-up New York. There were another 225 on the state's own remediation list. If the ratio of 2.25 state toxic sites to one federal Superfund toxic site holds up after all government tallies are completed, it would mean there are more than 100,000 places in the country toxic enough to seriously hurt local property values. By some estimates, there may actually be four times that number.

This does not include environmentally blighted sites that a government agency might not find objectionable but that would-be buyers invariably disdain. In this nebulous but nonetheless significant category are sites with an incinerator operating in the neighborhood or a nearby refinery that spews out fumes authorities classify as "offensive" but not "dangerous." Tap water with a chemical or fishy smell is another example of increasingly common environmental symptoms that may be more deleterious to property values than to health.

Beyond the rather obvious threats to home values are more subtle costs cropping up in the wake of progressive environmental decline. One big advantage home-owning used to enjoy over renting was the ability to control shelter costs. You paid your principal, interest, taxes and insurance. After that, except for emergency repairs, one's housing costs were more or less fixed.

The Cost to the Homeowner

Environmental problems are changing that. The villain here is local property taxes, which are going through the roof to pay for more costly solid-waste handling. The expense of shipping trash to landfills hundreds or even thousands of miles away has skyrocketed in many places.

Solid waste disposal costs in the Northeast rose from an average $20.59 a ton in 1986 to $39.23 a ton one year later. In 1988, property taxes jumped an average of 20 percent in Long Island, with much of this jump due to environmental expenses such as garbage disposal and asbestos removal from schools.

In at least one West Coast city, property owners are now charged by the barrel for trash the city collects. Such "user fees," of course, are actually another form of property tax. And, as every property owner knows, higher property taxes make selling a home more difficult.

Neighborhood pollution and the larger tax burden necessary to combat it are externals that negatively affect home values. Internals that bring down values are equally pervasive today.

The average American home is a toxic storehouse. It contains two to ten gallons of hazardous materials. Most of this is poured or flushed away over a period of time and ends up polluting the larger environment. Traces, however, end up tainting a house's own systems.

A more active risk than shelf toxics is caused by interior pollutants, such as radon, a naturally occurring radioactive gas. Radon contaminates an estimated 8 million American homes.

The results of radon scans are already affecting the price, even the salability, of residential properties, especially in the Northeast. One of the value-killing aspects of this kind of environmental hazard is that no one knows for sure what level of exposure to radon gas is dangerous. The EPA uses a standard of four picocuries of radon per liter of air. Some countries (for example, Canada) use a standard of 20 picocuries of radon per liter of air.

Without uniform and fixed standards, it becomes difficult for homeowners wishing to sell radon-tainted properties to know how much to spend to render them "safe." The cost of meeting one standard may be $1,500. Meeting a stricter standard may require spending $5,000 or more.

Making the wrong choice in such a situation can prove costly because repairs may have to be done twice. Theoretically, it could also expose buyers of properties that still bear some traces of radon to certain health risks, and sellers to down-the-road litigation risk.

Lead paint is another in-house toxic peril. It did not become illegal for interior use until 1971, and is therefore an undercoat in countless structures built before that year— in spite of concerted government efforts to find and scrape it away.

Asbestos linings around piping and water heaters is yet another widespread internal contaminant. Health concerns aside, the presence of any of these materials hurts when it comes to selling a property.

All environmental dangers property owners currently face in their own homes, of course, must also be confronted in second homes used for vacations or rented for income. To these are added the special environmental risks now associated with such locales as beaches and waterfronts.

A witness appearing before a congressional subcommittee recently summed up what would happen if ocean pollution around the nation were not sharply curtailed. "More beaches will close," he said. "Real estate values will go down."

That in a nutshell is exactly what occurred along the New Jersey shore in the summer of 1988. A survey of real estate salespeople in one county affected by New Jersey's offshore pollution found that 30 percent fewer buyers were in their area than the year before.

In addition to buildings, the raw land many Americans hold as an investment hedge is economically endangered, thanks to spreading pollution. In Vermont, for example, an environmentalist-inspired law puts a special tax on raw land that is resold in too short a time. The idea is to check development by making speculation less profitable.

Tract developers themselves are changing their way of doing business because of fears about environmental litigation. They are careful not to acquire virgin property that industrial dumpers might once have used on midnight runs. A spinoff of this new caution is that the profit potential of many individually owned undeveloped sites is reduced.

A new modified land-use plan announced in New Jersey in early 1988 offers another insight into how environmental considerations are changing the economics of raw land buying and selling. The head of the commission that formulated the statewide plan noted that one of its purposes was to check uncontrolled development "leading us to...environmental and social dead ends."

More people are affected by the growing environmental dangers associated with residential and "raw" properties than even direct ownership numbers suggest. This is because hundreds of thousands of nonhomeowners invest in residential developments through real estate limited partnerships (RELPs), real estate investment trusts (REITs), corporate pension funds, life insurance policies, etc.

The environmental sensitivity of professionals who run these institutions has risen dramatically in recent years. Indeed, one would be hard pressed to find a professional in this field today who does not take exceptional precautions to ensure that new property acquisitions meet strict environmental standards. Unfortunately, a good many of the acquisitions these newly sensitized professionals made prior to 1985 were not so carefully screened.

Much the same thing could be said about commercial and industrial properties now in the portfolios of these same large institutional investors. New environmental challenges to the economic worth of commercial structures and industrial developments are cropping up with alarming frequency.

A New Jersey statute, for example, forbids transferring ownership of industrial property without a strict audit that generates a clean environmental bill of health. As part of the nationwide trend to shift environmental costs from government to industry, the Massachusetts Department of Environmental Quality Engineering not so long ago proposed that owners of land deemed to be polluted pay the costs of the agency personnel overseeing its cleanup. Both these government moves hint at the growing costs and difficulties of owning "unclean" real estate.

There is an ex post facto clause in the U.S. Constitution that says that one cannot be tried for an offense that was not illegal at the time it was committed. This protection does not apply to environment-linked economic responsibilities. More and more, courts are taking the view that present owners of contaminated properties are responsible for cleaning up pollution introduced by former owners.

It is a concept with potentially mind-boggling consequences with respect to commercial and industrial property values.

When a historical society in Virginia did an environmental audit on a property it planned to acquire, lead and arsenic contamination were found in the basement. This sale-deadening discovery resulted from the fact that the site was an apothecaries shop in Colonial times.

A half-dozen states along the Eastern seaboard had major polluting industries operating within their borders by the late 18th century and another dozen Midwestern states by the 19th century. Dirty mining operations using highly toxic chemicals were as much a part of the Old West as Levi's® and sixguns. All such "historic" pollution could work to lower industrial and commercial property values in years to come.

A more recent—and far more dramatic—type of historic pollution that is challenging these same values involves asbestos. Between 1920 and the late 1970s, when the material was finally officially declared a health hazard, an estimated 768,000 structures were built using the material as insulation, or in soundproofing and fireproofing. A goodly percentage of all large office buildings that were built in this period contain some asbestos.

Asbestos abatement had become a $4-billion-a-year business by 1989. By 1993, it is expected to be an $11-billion-a-year activity. In all, it will likely cost upward of $100 billion to clear asbestos out of schools, where such work is federally mandated, apartment houses, and commercial and industrial structures covered by various state and local asbestos statutes. The effects on selling prices of privately owned structures have already been much affected by asbestos contamination.

Another facet of how *ex post facto* rules do not shield property owners from environmental liability can be seen in the ever-changing definitions of acceptable toxic thresholds. They are constantly being revised—almost always downward.

Thus, toxic levels that might have been permissible and not impaired a property's resale value could change overnight and turn a valuable asset into a white elephant. With the EPA now tracking some 500 indoor pollutants believed to be dangerous to human health, there seems no limit to potential economic risk here. With a 1976 federal law requiring companies to file reports on industrial toxics, and with a dozen states with even stricter disclosure requirements on the books, there also seems little way that these risks can be hidden from prospective buyers.

Environmental risks to commercial and industrial property owners take forms other than lower resale prices. An EPA study released in September 1988 chronicles the state of air quality in public buildings. The study's conclusions were not inspiring. Neither is the fact that 35,000 schools around the country will have to be cleansed of dangerous levels of asbestos, and perhaps half the nation's schools will have to receive some treatment for radon in classrooms. The EPA itself was reported to be operating a tainted building in late 1988—a place where employees suffered various discomforts related to indoor contamination. All these findings, hinting at the widespread nature of environmental real estate problems in public structures, suggest the extent to which owners of large private structures could be affected by the same problems.

"Sick-building syndrome," as this newly discovered malady has been dubbed, has generated no major court awards at the time of this writing. But it is one of those sleeper liabilities with a potential that present and future owners of commercial property must consider.

Before looking at ways property owners can protect themselves from environmental shock, it might be noted that like all widespread challenges to established values, this one bears within itself some interesting peripheral opportunities. Radon in the basement is viewed by millions of homeowners as an injurious presence but as a beneficial presence by thousands of arthritis sufferers who annually visit radon-pervaded "health mines."

In a less suspect vein, there are literally scores of small rural communities in the South and Midwest queuing up to accept overflow solid waste of large Eastern cities. If these new final resting places for burgeoning urban waste are properly and safely constructed (which was often not the case in years past), they might come to represent important new sources of revenue for badly strapped communities—and for a few local landowners in these communities.

Self-Defense for Home Buyers

A later chapter discusses how business executives can protect their firms' commercial and industrial properties from environmental risk. Here, we focus on what homeowners and prospective homeowners can do to achieve the same end.

The first step in this process is to evaluate the *external* environmental exposure of a piece of real estate, i.e., the air, water and soil risks in the neighborhood (and perhaps in the town or city) where a piece of land or a building is located.

The local health department is a good place to start. Every health department in the country has been informed about sites in its own area on the EPA's National Priority List. State health departments can usually supply information about other federally and state-listed Superfund sites as well. A full listing of all licensed landfills in the country, whether presently considered hazardous or not, can be obtained from the EPA.

One can get some notion of general water quality in a particular locale by contacting municipal water districts or departments of health. They will generally be able to supply up-to-date facts about chemicals and other known contaminants in local drinking water.

Data on local air quality standards is available from the EPA. The agency monitors the air nationwide, and each of its 11 regional offices can supply facts about violations within its own jurisdiction. Similar information can be obtained from state air compliance offices. Facts of this kind have special significance to people who already suffer from breathing disorders (asthma, bronchitis, etc.), as well as people with especially sensitive skin.

One quick way to get up to date on the environmental health of an area you may not be familiar with is to read a year's back copies of the local newspaper. During the 1980s, when the "big press" was obligingly accepting an official view that an ignored environment was a healthy environment, the "little press" became the best source of news in this field. In many respects it still is.

In lieu of actually visiting the office of a local weekly and poring over back issues, a conversation with the editor is often most helpful. If he or she is not also a real estate agent, this is an excellent way to learn about the extent of local environmental problems.

A similar shortcut involves contacting the person in charge of the local Sierra Club or Greenpeace chapter. Aside from information about local environmental concerns, these people may provide insights into local zoning boards' attitudes toward variances that could harm an area's future appeal to property owners.

A person's own observational skills are often helpful in spotting external environmental threats to a property's worth. Just as a would-be buyer will walk or drive around a house to see where the nearest shops are located, environmental audit walks and drives can be enlightening.

Is there a leaking tank under the abandoned gas station on the corner? What was the old woodlot up the road used for, and why do all the trees on the property look so sickly? What source feeds the water in the pond? What did the old factory at the edge of town manufacture before it went out of business? Any number of questions like these can emerge from an audit walk or drive.

Beyond hunting out environmental deterioration in all its varied forms, value-conscious real estate shoppers should also be keenly aware of the environmental "positives" that can boost the resale price of their properties in years to come. One such positive is proximity to national, state or private trust conservation land.

Federal land-banking languished in the Reagan years. The Land and Water Conservation Fund, established by Congress in 1965 and supported by a tax on oil drilling on the continental shelf, spent only $206 million to purchase land for conservation purposes in 1988, down from $509 million spent in 1980.

Such purchases, however, may well increase during the Bush Administration. In addition, state land conservation purchase programs are flourishing, especially in the crowded Northeast, where New York, New Jersey and Connecticut together have allocated more than $600 million to buy land for their state reserves.

In terms of private activities in this realm, more than 350 new land trusts have been formed since 1980 alone. The primary function of these organizations is to buy land and remove it from the development pool.

Real estate professionals and small town government officials have traditionally regarded "land banking" as a bad thing for local property values because when the scope of private development in a given area is limited, fewer developers come in and bid up tract prices.

Those attuned to the environmental factor, however, understand that in a world where environmental deterioration is progressing at an alarming rate, the more local land that is not "developed" or developable, the higher the future prices of local property are likely to be. Increasingly, the absence of past development, which forces property tax boosts to pay for expensive waste disposal services, and the future impossibility of such development because of nearby conservancy tracts are what kick up local property values.

The maturing relationship of unspoiled, "woodsy" environments to heightened property values was explored in a story that appeared in the gardening section of *The New York Times* in February 1989. It reported that "research conducted by the United States Forest Service showed that trees can contribute an average of 7 percent to the value of a half-acre home site and as much as 27 percent of the appraised value of the property."

Clearly, when it come to residential property buying these days, good local environments and the presence of unspoiled nature are strong inducements.

Along with a home's setting with respect to the external environment, its *internal* environmental risks should be carefully evaluated by would-be buyers. Part of this job can be done by the same people who do prepurchase home inspections. Many of these specialists now do radon tests, look for asbestos and scrape for lead paint, at the same time that they check the plumbing and seek out leaks in the roof. A few will send tap water samples to a lab for an extra charge.

When it comes to internal environments, too, a little personal initiative can often prove useful. If every house you visit in a given neighborhood uses bottled water, for example, it might signify something worth checking.

It also pays to ask about possible indoor pollution from carpeting material you can see and insulating materials that are hidden. If basement fans and blowers indicate the house was once contaminated with radon, it will probably behoove you to see that this system is still in good working order.

Steps that individuals take to protect their real estate investments by employing the environmental factor have considerable social utility, as well as merit from the perspective of personal finance. Put simply, they work to reward present owners who have used sound environmental practices with respect to their properties and to penalize owners who allowed their structures or their surroundings to suffer environmental harm.

Homeowners who become active on local zoning boards or participate in town meetings to prevent the introduction of environmentally harmful "development" in their communities are working toward good social as well as good personal ends. They are practicing a kind of pocketbook environmentalism with beneficial overall consequences.

Some readers might discern an undemocratic edge in these views—a justification for those-that-have to see that those-who-need are denied a chance to move up. But this misses the point when it comes to the sea change that has occurred in recent years when it comes to the relationship of the environment to the economy as a whole.

Unbridled economic development no longer expands the financial horizons of the many at the expense of quality-of-life for the few. That may have been the case in years past. But today, the costs of pollution associated with unbridled real estate development actually fall hardest on people least able to pay them.

Property development beyond a certain point in environmentally "saturated" areas brings fewer economic benefits in terms of jobs and housing opportunities and greater economic burdens in the form of waste disposal, health problems and the like. The democratic response to such development, the response with the most economic advantages for the most people, is to keep overdevelopment from occurring.

Property owners working to check development are thus practicing a new populism, not perpetuating an old-fashioned elitism.

CHAPTER 6

The Environmental
Factor and Stocks

When most people think of "environmental investments," they think of common stocks of pollution control and solid-waste management companies. This is a narrow view of environmental investing, of course, but it encompasses a field that can yield positive returns for those who intelligently employ the environmental factor and is, therefore, worth exploring in some detail.

One popular annual directory lists some 2,500 manufacturers of environmental products and equipment and more than 3,000 environmental consulting companies. The environmental universe followed by Wall Streeters, however, is much smaller. It consists of about 80 publicly traded stocks, the majority sold over the counter.

From the perspective of most professional stock traders, the only "environmental stocks" are those issued by companies whose sole or primary business is providing an easily recognized pollution-control product or service. Beyond this, institutional professionals with a lot of money to invest usually only follow companies with fairly large "floats."

Float refers to how widely ownership of a company's common share is distributed. Stocks too narrowly held—i.e., that have too small a float—make it hard for would-be institutional and other large-block stock traders to find a buyer or seller when the need arises.

This Wall Street criterion for environmental stocks suitable for professional consideration was so restrictive that until the mid-1980s, it encompassed no more than a dozen or so companies like Waste Management, Inc.; Browning-Ferris Industries, Inc.; and Zurn Industries, Inc. Few brokerage firms even had in-house environmental services specialists before the middle part of this decade. Most covered the field (if at all) by assigning pollution control and analysis duties to someone who spent most of his or her time evaluating transportation or energy stocks.

In recent years, a fair number of brokerage houses and other institutions have expanded their regular tracking of older environmental services companies to include such firms as Roy F. Weston, Inc., Riedel Environmental Services and Canonie Environmental Services Corp. They have also broadened their definition of firms that fit into this group, adding companies like Calgon Carbon, Davis Water & Waste and Betz Laboratories. Some relative newcomers to the ranks of publicly traded companies, like Clean Harbors, are now regularly followed by analysts as well.

Wall Street's Heightened Interest

The recent heightened interest by Wall Street in environmental stocks is directly related to the public reaction to the environmental scares of the summer of 1988. During the third quarter of 1988, this reaction made the pollution-control group of stocks the best performing in the market, with individual companies in the group averaging stock price rises of 20 percent and 30 percent. A new administration in Washington with a stronger environmental protection bent and well-publicized new regulations pertaining to solid-waste management and groundwater contamination worked to further boost environmental stock prices in this period.

By early 1989, the public interest in environmental service companies was so strong that several specialized newsletters focusing on the field were being successfully marketed. That surefire Wall Street barometer of pop trends, Merrill Lynch, was also offering a special report entitled "Cleaning Up Our Polluted Planet: Investment Opportunities in Pollution Control."

Should people employing the environmental factor add some of Wall Street's traditional environmental "plays" to their personal stock portfolios? Almost certainly.

As a group, these investors will benefit from the inevitable continuation of environmental deterioration that is bound to occur in years to come. The prices of their stocks will tend to bubble up whenever an especially nasty environmental scare jolts the national consciousness. Many environmental service companies have been among the fastest growing stocks of the entire American economy in recent years, with annual growth rates of 30 percent to 40 percent in a commonplace. (See the table of some popular stocks on the next page.)

An article in the January 25, 1989, issue of *Focus Magazine* summed up the thinking of many investment professionals when it closed with the words: "...today it is no exaggeration to suggest that waste management may turn out to be the 'glamour industry' of the 1990s."

This is not to say, of course, that all of the billions and billions of dollars that will go into environment-related rehabilitation in years to come will necessarily end up in the

Recent Performances of Some
Well-Known Environmental Services Companies

Name of Company	Traded on (Symbol)	Main Business*	1988 Revenues,† Net Income (Loss)	1987 Revenues, Net Income (Loss)	Revenue Percentage Change‡
Allwaste, Inc.	NASDAQ (ALWS)	Hazardous-waste mgt.	$ 67,804,000 5,329,000	$ 45,894,000 2,667,000	+49%
The Brand Companies	NASDAQ (BRAN)	Asbestos abatement	163,812,000 4,488,000	116,583,000 (4,089,000)	+40%
Browning-Ferris Industries, Inc.	NYSE (BFI)	Solid-waste mgt.	2,067,405,000 226,864,300	1,656,616,000 172,025,000	+25%
Canonie Environmental Services Corp.	NASDAQ (CANO)	Hazardous-waste mgt.	48,004,000 9,047,000	39,302,000 11,385,000	+22%
Chambers Development Company Corp.	AMEX (CDVB)	Solid-waste mgt.	137,040,000 20,736,000	58,785,000 10,030,180	+133%
Groundwater Technology, Inc.	NASDAQ (GWTI)	Water treatment	66,141,000 6,146,000	37,153,000 3,381,000	+78%
Gundle Environmental Systems, Inc.	AMEX (GUN)	Landfill liners	88,871,000 6,517,000	50,448,000 3,164,000	+76%
Rollins Environmental Services, Inc.	NYSE (REN)	Hazardous-waste mgt.	206,285,000 33,331,000	173,619,000 28,393,000	+19%
Versar, Inc.	AMEX (VSR)	Hazardous-waste mgt.	52,450,000 (1,567,000)	43,607,000 825,000	+20%
Waste Management, Inc.	NYSE (WMX)	Solid-waste mgt.	3,565,617,000 464,223,000	2,757,630,000 327,078,000	+29%
Roy F. Weston, Inc.	NASDAQ (WSTNA)	Hazardous-waste mgt.	194,878,000 1,898,000	137,091,000 4,579,000	+20%
Zurn Industries, Inc.	NYSE ZRN	Water treatment	405,756,000 19,153,000	383,306,000 17,740,000	+ 6%

*Many environmental services companies are full-service and active in different kinds of cleanup work.

†These are fiscal year, not calendar year, totals.

‡Depending on individual circumstances, some companies on this table had good years in terms of net income and some not-so-good years. But as these year-to-year revenue change percentages show, almost all did a lot more business. This suggests the general growth in the environmental services industry.

coffers of Wall Street's present environmental favorites. Much of this money will actually go to companies described later in this chapter as "secondary environmental plays" or to the fast-growing environmental cleanup subsidiaries of some of this country's biggest polluters.

Thus, while recognizing the potential in a portfolio of environmental stocks, people who wish to get the most out of Wall Street's environmental "pure plays" must exercise a certain amount of intelligence. At a minimum, they should understand the peculiar nature of the environmental services industry as presently defined by the brokerage community, understand the different sectors that make up that industry and appreciate the difficulties, as well as the opportunities, faced by each sector.

The industry itself is very young. "Old-timers" here are companies like Roy F. Weston, Inc., which got into the business in 1955. Most companies presently attracting the interest of investors were incorporated (or at least substantially restructured) in the years since 1984. This means, among other things, that lengthy track records on which to base investment judgments are frequently lacking in this field.

The phenomenal growth records chalked up by some environmental companies do not always reflect real increases in business. Acquisition has been the order of the day in this realm in the past few years. Bigger revenues from year to year have, therefore, not always been matched by higher net earnings. Sometimes management's abilities have lagged behind a corporation's physical growth, leading to unpleasant stock price dips after a few high-flying years.

Overall, the U.S. environmental service industry is the largest in the world and the most technically advanced. More than one-half of one percent of this country's entire GNP goes into meeting environmental problems—a sum that may not sound large, until compared to the runner-up in the world, West Germany, which spends only about one-third of one percent of its GNP on such outlays, and Japan, which spends about one-tenth of one percent.

Such expenditures have created a surprisingly high-tech industry, very different from the pick-up-the-trash, dump-the-55-gallon-drum image many people still have of environmental services. From an investment perspective, this high-tech operation brings in its train added investment risks related to such things as the threat of obsolescence. Put simply: The day another company comes out with a better way to dispose of the waste your company has been handling profitably could be the day you take a bath in the market.

The Basics

In broadest terms, environmental services companies are involved in air-pollution control, water treatment, hazardous-waste management, or some combination of the three. Within these categories, firms focus on testing and analysis, collecting, transporting, recycling, burning, burying or chemically transforming wastes and other pollutants.

There are special tribulations associated with each of these activities. But a major variable for all is the flow of government funding of cleanup projects, which tends to be not only irregular but also less than officially announced figures might lead one to believe.

Though Superfund allocations between 1986 and 1991 are supposed to total $8.5 billion, for example, just $300 million was actually spent in 1987. Firms expecting to cash in on a "Superfund bonanza" have thus far been disappointed. Similar disappointments could lie ahead for other environmental services hopefuls counting on government largesse.

Bigger federal budgets to clean the environment do not always translate into more business for private environmental firms. Recent calls for the EPA to perform more testing and evaluation work in-house may or may not improve the quality of hazardous-waste handling. But it will *certainly* work to reduce revenues of companies that depend on EPA contracts.

State spending on environmental cleanup rose sharply to about $3 billion in 1987. But the level of this spending, too, could well drop in the near future because some environmentally active states, like Massachusetts, Pennsylvania and New Jersey, are now feeling budgetary squeezes.

With about one half of the largest cities in this country facing serious problems balancing their own budgets, it would be surprising indeed if direct new municipal spending initiatives boosting revenues of environmental services companies were inaugurated. Rising interest rates and a less-than-vital municipal bond market may also rein in borrowing for local cleanup projects.

Another potential check on environmental service company profits comes from increased competition in certain industry sectors. Activities like asbestos abatement and testing and analysis have what are termed "low capital thresholds," which means it is relatively easy for new competitors to enter the field. Generally speaking, the more competition, the smaller the margins and the company profits.

The Bane of the Industry

The biggest thorn for environmental services industry as a whole is probably the legal liability so closely bound up with environmental cleanup work. Society's honey carriers tend to drop tidbits off their carts in the course of a day's work. And our society is very intolerant of failings in this regard.

Environmental services firms are thus among the most frequent recipients of government fines and penalties. Because the realities of modern waste disposal dictate that many toxic substances are not permanently neutralized but simply changed into less toxic forms or moved to less dangerous sites, this liability will remain a constant in the field for some time to come.

Making this liability even more serious for environmental service firms is the increasing difficulty of hedging it with insurance. One of the many inconsistencies of government policy toward control of pollution is that federal and state bureaucracies, following legislative mandates, demand that companies that clean a tainted site be financially at risk for their work, while the courts render judgments so large for failure to perform jobs correctly that no insurer will underwrite coverage of many cleanup projects.

A consequence of this situation is that many environmental firms are actually self-insured—often through a wholly owned insurance subsidiary. The profit-killing potential in such a setup could be very real indeed under certain circumstances.

Once prospective investors understand some of the drawbacks as well as the opportunities of environmental investing the Wall Street way, they can begin stock picking. Almost any broker these days will be happy to provide a list of environmental companies favored by his firm's own analysts. Based on the above caveats, here are some things to consider when narrowing down the choices.

Since so many federal and local agencies, legislatures and courts can now pass laws, rulings and decisions that affect an environmental company's bottom line, you may want to invest in a company that has diversified environmental operations. If it becomes easier to burn waste than bury it, for example, a company in both businesses is covered, while one that is too specialized may be hurt. Similar patterns apply in many environmental services sectors.

If one invests in a company that is more specialized, its products or services should enjoy a solid technological or bureaucratic edge over the competition. An example of the former might be a patent on a safe, cheap technique to dispose of a common, dangerous toxic material. Examples of the later include a state license to operate a much-needed facility such as a low-level nuclear waste repository.

It is wise to remember when evaluating an environmental services firm that its true worth is often closely related to the locations and license status of its real estate. In many respects, in fact, solid-waste management is just a fancy term for a trucking business with extensive property (dump) holdings. Hazardous-waste management is largely a business of owning licensed waste-handling preserves, and defending one's licenses against endless nitpicking.

While fines and penalties may financially cripple some environmental companies, they may be just a part of the regular overhead for others. One simple way to get a handle on which applies to a prospective investment vehicle is to check its prospectus or annual report, seeking notes on court judgments, fines and similar liabilities.

A million-dollar fine levied against a company with $10 million in annual revenues is serious. A dozen hundred-thousand-dollar fines levied against a firm with hundreds of millions in annual revenues are like parking tickets to an overnight carrier.

In checking the lawsuits section of the annual report, *pending suits* should be carefully considered. Losing a big one here could be financially fatal for some firms.

One important caution investors should note on the matter of fines and the environmental service companies that get them: while appreciating that some pollution citations may be an unavoidable part of this business, beware direct descendants of the "midnight dumpers." Some smaller firms traded over the counter still fit in this nasty category. They thrive briefly by taking the waste no one else wants, unloading it the cheapest way possible, then waxing fat for the years and years it sometimes takes for the American legal system to bring them to ground.

Such companies and their managers are not only vexatious to the spirit but represent a very real investment risk for people who buy their shares. The same firm founders who dump on the environment have a tendency to milk their corporate creations dry, leaving nothing for investors to salvage but a flood of injunctions.

The source of a company's revenues, as well as its size, is important. Some companies that do a lot of government work may prosper in years to come. But because there is a growing trend for government to pass along environmental cleanup costs to corporate America, firms servicing private customers will likely profit more than government contractors in the future.

In gauging the worth of an environmental service company's corporate customer base, of course, Fortune 500 companies are always the customer base of choice. Big corporations pay their environmental debts to contractors and suppliers. Smaller ones often go into bankruptcy when these costs get too onerous.

Secondary Plays

Dabbling in the relatively restrictive universe of pure plays currently favored by Wall Street professionals need not be the only way for individuals to invest in environmental cleanup. The simple perception that hundreds and hundreds of public companies outside this universe also

stand to benefit directly from changing government policies and public tastes opens up enormously wider investing horizons.

Consider the many public companies, large and small,
now active in recycling. The demand for one of the long-
time pillars of this market, newsprint, was soft in early
1989 because additional supplies were becoming available
faster than new demand. New recycling regulations taking hold in many cities contributed to this glut. But the
long-term prospects for companies recycling paper and a
host of other materials will make this sector one of the
real growth areas in the next decade's economy.

Between 1970 and 1988, the amount of paper recycled
in this country more than doubled, to 26.5 million tons a
year, and American exports of recycled paper jumped
more than tenfold, to 5.5 million tons a year. The amount
of nonpaper material rescued from municipal landfills by
recycling in 1988 was 15 million tons, compared with less
than half that amount in 1970.

Plastic recycling is on the verge of becoming a very big
business. Currently, plastics—which account for about
seven percent of this country's solid-waste stream but, because of their bulk, take up some 30 percent of fast-
disappearing landfill space—are recycled in miniscule
amounts.

Of the 10.5 million tons of plastic waste generated in
1988, only 100,000 tons or so were recycled. More than five
times that amount is expected to be recycled by the mid-
1990s, according to industry sources.

The 2 billion old tires in this country are no longer just
an eyesore in litter piles and empty lots. They can now be
retreaded, converted into fuel, or turned into literally hundreds of nontransportation products.

In some places and at certain seasons, there is strong
competition for existing tire stocks. A number of pulp and
paper mills, for example, use pelletized rubber as fuel

during the winter. Recycled tires also go into making railroad ties and are being tested as a substitute road resurfacing material.

The economic potential of recycling—whether paper, plastics, metals, glass, solvents, rubber or whatever—is extraordinary. Chapter 11, on entrepreneurial opportunities, explores it from another standpoint.

Here, one need only remember that along with the corporate giants, like Waste Management, Inc., which are making a major commitment in this field, a great many smaller, newer public companies are cropping up to take advantage of society's need to dispose of its trash more efficiently. Some may be worth considering by people employing the environmental factor.

Environmental Self-Help

Another group of companies that fit in this secondary-plays category are manufacturers of what might be called "environmental self-defense products." The best-known items in this line presently are home-testing kits for radon. Many such kits are now being marketed.

The reason is not hard to fathom. Radon, a naturally radioactive gas, is thought to be responsible for 5,000 to 20,000 cancer deaths each year. As many as a third of the homes tested in six states—North Dakota, Minnesota, Pennsylvania, Massachusetts, Missouri and Arizona—showed traces of the gas. Some officials estimate 8 million American homes in all may be contaminated. This has created a boom for radon test-kit manufacturers.

Other types of environmental self-defense products are also proliferating. They include radiation detectors for people concerned about residues from local nuclear facilities, fiberoptic and chemical sensors that can detect dangerous substances near suspected toxic sites, and a slew of gadgets one attaches to faucets to make the liquids coming out of them less offensive.

The biggest single environmental self-defense product being sold today, however, and one with considerable possibilities for stock investors, is probably bottled water. This is currently a $2-billion-a-year market, and its phenomenal recent growth of late is directly related to the public's growth fear of what is in our drinking water.

Fueling this fear are stories like the one that appeared in *The New York Times* in May 1988. Under the headline, "Puzzling Findings on Bottled Water in Pregnancy," this article discussed studies about miscarriages in California.

"In the four studies," it noted, "the rate of miscarriages in women who reported drinking no tap water during pregnancy ranged from zero to 7.7 percent. The rate for women who drank at least some tap water ranged from 8.4 to 13.1 percent...The rate of birth defects in the children of tap water drinkers was 2.6 percent to 6.2 percent, while the rate for those who drank no tap water was zero to 1.6 percent. The expected rate was 2 to 3 percent."

Most investors would not be surprised to read that the biggest company in terms of bottled water sales in 1988 was the Perrier Group. Some, however, might find it interesting that the Clorox Company is also a major participant in this market. Suntory International (known for alcoholic beverages) is still another active player in this field, while beer giant Adolph Coors Co. is also moving into sparkling waters in a big way. Bottled water, in fact, is now the fastest growing part of the U.S. beverage industry.

Peripheral Investing Vision

There are many secondary environmental plays other than recycling and self-defense product plays. The use of the environmental factor to discover investments with rich payback potential, in fact, is limited only by a person's imagination.

Once you begin asking questions like "What frightens me most about environmental deterioration?" and "Which companies seem to be doing something to alleviate my fears?" you are already quantum leaps ahead of Wall Streeters who view pollution control as just another interesting little niche in the industrial stock index. Once you develop this peripheral vision, you are ready to examine the full range of environmental investing opportunities.

One could give countless examples of ways that the environmental factor can be used to spot future stock winners in areas that might otherwise escape notice. A look at the energy industry illustrates the point. In an earlier chapter we looked at how investors in energy companies with large environmental exposure could be hurt in years to come. The other side of this equation is that certain producers and suppliers of energy and energy-related systems will enjoy an edge in a world where increasing attention must be paid to protecting natural systems.

Environment-linked energy plays can include everything from backing firms making low-polluting transportation vehicles to those engineering high-efficiency cogeneration systems. The three best-known environmental energy plays just now, however, are fusion, natural gas and solar energy.

The first has no "investable" opportunities at the time of this writing, in spite of all the talk in the press about "cold fusion." The second is a very complicated play, with profits of gas-producing companies and pipelines likely to be determined as much by the cohesion of foreign cartels and the oddball perambulations of federal energy regulators as by environmental needs.

While natural gas itself burns clean, natural gas *firms* may subject the environment to their own brand of environmental insults. One of the largest was recently fined several hundred million dollars for PCB droppings deposited along its pipelines in 14 states.

Power From the Sun

The solar environmental play, though limited in scope, is more straightforward. It provides a clearer example of the still speculative but, in light of growing concerns about the environment, increasingly interesting investment opportunities for people who employ the environmental factor.

Solar energy holds a unique place in American economic history. The attempts of the federal government to promote solar technologies in the wake of the 1973 Arab Oil Embargo constitute what is almost certainly the classic case study of how befuddled legislators and out-of-control bureaucrats, prodded by well-meaning activists without the slightest understanding of how free markets operate, can temporarily ruin an industry.

All the ingredients were in place for a major solar revolution during the 1970s. Solar heating systems were technically simple and, in the case of solar water heaters, had been commercially manufactured for 50 years. The public was enamored of the concept of energy from the sun and anxious to buy in. Price differentials between solar energy and more conventional carbon fuels need not have held back wide-scale consumer acceptance any more than higher natural gas prices in the 1930s and 1940s kept people from purchasing what was then being marketed as the "ultimate clean fuel."

What did cripple the fledgling solar energy industry in the 1970s was a Congress that promised tax credits for five years but failed to deliver any because these credits became a hostage in debates about taxing the oil industry. A federal bureaucracy incapable of dealing with simple technology also did its share to undermine the solar revolution by promoting and publicizing the most exotic and least practical solar applications imaginable, convincing most Americans in the process that solar energy was a 21st-century resource.

A fringe of consumer protection crazies finished the job on solar energy in the late 1970s. These well-meaning zealots fantasized a need to protect buyers from "fast-buck schemers," and were so successful in convincing would-be solar product purchasers of the need to wait for elaborate warrantees and for government standards to be set that most solar manufacturers went out of business while confused customers dawdled.

Had the public been as "well protected" from the early pitches of stereo system manufacturers, we would still be listening to monaural recordings. Early stereo systems were as big as dishwashers, had the words HI-FI prominently displayed on their front panels, and cost about $1,200 when they first appeared in the 1950s. You might say that everyone who bought these early systems was "bilked," in the sense that you can buy stereo units today that give ten times the sound at one-tenth the cost in inflation-adjusted dollars. Because there were no consumer-protectors around in the 1950s to shield people from making such purchases, however, the market developed to the benefit of manufacturers and consumers alike.

If the public had been forcefully shielded from the hype of first-generation personal computer manufacturers, word processing, too, would still be done with carbon paper and liquid whitener. The first PCs to appear in the 1970s were so expensive that one model was highlighted in the same Nieman-Marcus catalog that featured a family zoo. Both items were aimed exclusively at big spenders. Again, you could say anyone who bought early PCs was cheated, because infinitely better products are available today at a fraction of the cost. But this is so only because early product lines were not monitored by "consumer protectors."

Mercifully, some elements of the solar energy industry managed to survive the ministrations of well-intentioned legislators and consumer advocates. Unfortunately, this remnant still had to pass through the Internal Revenue Service's sieve.

There were no federal tax credits between 1975 and 1980 because of congressional deal-making. Between 1980 and 1985, when such credits *were* available, their potentially positive effect on sales of solar energy goods was considerably lessened because eager-beaver IRS agents were canvassing the country, making sure no "fast-buck schemers" or their customers were cheating the government out of unseemly amounts of tax revenue.

The federal government's direct solar budget has fallen from almost $600 million in 1980 to less than $100 million today. In recent years, with the winding down of tax credits, the IRS has been removed as a factor in the solar-energy market. Solar's little helpers have also lost interest in the technology.

The result? As solar energy has finally stopped being a movement and become a mere market, a few solar manufacturers have again started to look like attractive investment vehicles.

Passive solar heating designs and accessories are now readily available and are being incorporated into many new and existing buildings in the southern part of the country. Active solar heating systems are state-of-the-art. In the all-important area of solar-generated power using photovoltaic cells, efficiency levels and mass manufactur-

ing techniques are on the verge of making important mar
ket breakthroughs.

Already, U.S.-manufactured photovoltaic cells are a
$100-million-a-year industry, with more than half of this
in export sales. Thanks to a reduced federal presence in
this field (federal photovoltaic expenditures dropped from
$150 million in 1981 to less than $25 million in 1988), the
United States now leads the world in this technology.

Photovoltaic cells are used to power hundreds of products, from watches to calculators to patio lights to novelty
items of every shape and description. Of far greater importance, the same cells are running communication and
lighting equipment in areas where regular power lines are
not economically feasible.

With the efficiency of some photovoltaic cells nearing
15 percent and predictions that 30 percent efficiency may
be imminent, sometime, in the not-too-distant future,
banks of these cells may be used by utilities to handle part
of their peak-load power demands. In this regard, it is
worth noting that the per-watt cost of solar power has
fallen to one-tenth what it was a decade ago. Successful
development of "thin film" technology, which substitutes
coated glass for silicon wafers, could expedite even
steeper manufacturing cuts.

Batteries that will one day store commercial solar-
generated electrical power have undergone their own
technical revolution in recent years. And better batteries
make off-the-grid solar homes an immediate economic
possibility.

Companies that make free-market solar products are
the sort of investment that might appeal to people who understand the importance of the environmental factor.
When these people ask the question: "What frightens
me?" the answer comes back, "Tainted air." Solar heating
and electric generation do not taint the air.

Similar questions about a growing number of companies and industries are being asked and answered by people who understand the investment uses of the environmental factor.

The Hedge

Before passing on to the role environmental deterioration plays in bond and commodity investing, one final point must be emphasized with respect to the environmental factor and stocks. It is that the environmental factor should be used not only to spot opportunities that generate profits but also as a means to hedge against stock losses as well.

Smart stock owners periodically make decisions to cull their holdings based on changing market attitudes toward inflation, interest rates and recession. Whether this is done annually or semiannually, whether one's personal portfolio is large or small, such regular evaluations should also include "environmental audits" of all stocks in light of prevailing or expected new market conditions.

There are all sorts of things such audits might consider. Many are directly related to the specific business activities of companies being evaluated. Some general things to look for, however, and some basic approaches to getting economically significant environmental facts an investor needs are applicable in most situations.

Investors, for example, will almost always want to consider the general environmental exposure of the industry on which their money is riding. Sometimes the profit prognosis for an entire industry can change overnight because of a single bureaucratic or court ruling.

A court decision concerning the insurance industry's liabilities with respect to certain environmental damages may affect future profits of dozens of insurers. New rules with respect to a category of toxic substances might place a profit-killing burden on every firm in a given manufacturing industry. Stiffer standards in reporting environmental cleanup costs might wipe millions of dollars in equity off the balance sheets of some petrochemical companies.

Of course, wise investors know that not all companies in an industry suffer equally from an industrywide threat to profits. They also realize that a heavier environmental burden, in and of itself, does not necessarily make an industry and its components unattractive to investors. The chemical industry as a whole, for example, has been booming in recent years, in spite of its growing environmental burdens.

Still, applying the environmental factor in a broad way when making a regular portfolio audit can save one from some nasty future surprises. Consider what happened to the stock price of all asbestos producers after word about the environmental dangers of that substance began to emerge and lawsuits began to be initiated.

Beyond general, industrywide aspects of an environmental audit, one should focus on the environmental exposure and performance of individual corporations. What are some things to look for? Ask the following questions:

- Does a firm have a history of being challenged in court on environmental matters and is it currently involved in such litigation?
- Does a company own the kind of real estate that might expose it to expensive remediation costs in the future? Property in this category may include abandoned heavy industrial sites, as well as nuclear and chemical facilities.
- How much did a company spend to rid itself of internally generated toxic materials in the past

year, and how did this stack up with the year before? If the jump was very great, even bigger outlays may be necessary in years ahead. Whether or not a company is building reserves to cover this type of expense in the future is an issue analysts and investors alike might consider.

These are a few of the questions raised by awareness of the environmental factor. Getting the answers is often a lot easier than one might suppose. Individual investors can often get by with a bit of reading and a phone call or two.

Prospectuses for new stocks frequently have sections dealing with pending environmental matters. Some—but by no means all—annual reports are beginning to feature similar information.

A call to one's stockbroker may elicit facts about a company's environmental exposure that the brokerage firm's research department has garnered. A call to the investor services department of a company in which one is interested can usually produce even more immediate information.

Calls to companies should focus on specific facts that an investor (or would-be investor) feels are genuinely relevant to a decision whether to buy or not to buy a stock. The answers one receives should be both specific and straightforward.

If one accepts the importance of the environmental factor in determining how well companies in various industries will perform in the future, one expects firms entrusted with investment capital to appreciate it, too. Hints that they do not may affect decisions about where to park one's money.

One of the nice things about undertaking a personal environmental stock audit is that it not only protects and enhances a person's own wealth, it has considerable social utility. It is actually one way the environmental factor works to improve the environment.

The first reaction of most large American corporations to environmental queries is to treat them as public relations exercises. Covers of annual reports begin to feature neat and unobtrusive corporate facilities in bucolic settings. The company's name starts appearing on lists of corporate donors to wildlife associations. Investor relations departments are beefed up with people who give carefully programmed answers whenever the word "environment" is mentioned.

It would be a mistake, however, to underestimate the influence of persistent, widespread, investor-initiated market environmentalism on corporate America. If a load of old teabags in the morning mail could force a reluctant U.S. Congress to back down on pay raises its members wanted desperately, strong evidence that a lot of investors were thinking of bailing out of a stock might well hasten company moves into more responsible actions vis-à-vis the environment.

After all, much of the personal wealth of top corporate executives is represented by stock in their own companies, or by options to buy such stock. For very strong personal reasons, they do not want to see their company's share prices go down.

Investors using the environmental factor are sending a message to these people. The message is that the environment is not only quality of life. It is also raw economics: the *investor's* personal economics; the *executive's* personal economics; the *company's* economics.

This is the sort of message that is understood by executives in every industry.

CHAPTER 7

The Environmental Factor and Bonds

Once upon a time, bonds were the sure solace of widows and orphans and the dependable financial shield that protected well-endowed coupon-clippers from the indignities of honest toil. No longer.

A casino mentality has come to the bond market. Speculation and volatility are now part and parcel of securities that are not supposed to exhibit either.

In terms of outright risk, bonds are still considerably less chancy as investment vehicles than stocks or commodities. But such a direct comparison overlooks a crucial difference that should be very high on the list of investor priorities: risk-reward ratios.

While it is true that you can lose all your capital investing in commodities and most of it investing in a stock that goes sour, you can also double or triple a stock investment within a relatively short period, and do even better if a commodity deal hits perfectly. With bonds the capital upside is far more limited. Thus, if an investor gives up too much in the way of safety for a shot at this limited upside potential, the risk-reward tradeoff can be most unfavorable

The Bond Fund Dilemma

Such an unfavorable tradeoff now exists for many people who own bonds directly or own them "passively" through mutual funds, life insurance policies or pension systems. It exists because of three major changes that have occurred in bond markets in recent years.

The first is that these markets have evolved into something they were never intended to be—a "sponge" to soak up excess dollars and other currencies that governments cannot stop pumping out at record rates. Instead of current inflation, the enormous new volume of paper money now being printed is transformed into future debt obligations. To put this another way, it is converted from present to deferred inflation.

The second reason is that various national and international mechanisms have caused this excess store of new money to be lumped together in enormous capital pools managed by people with little more than a theoretical personal responsibility for their bond-buying decisions— and, often, strong personal interests in investing in a risky manner.

Multibillion-dollar pension funds are an excellent example of how this accretion of funds increases bond risk. There are few rewards for pension fund managers who take the long view appropriate to meeting the 21st-century needs of their client pensioners. There are excellent short-term bonus benefits for fund managers who buy riskier bond issues that pay higher near-term dividends.

It makes the numbers on their quarterly reports look better. This, in turn, works to boost this year's management compensation packages. By the time a shaky bond deal collapses, in two or three years, the parties responsible for hurting bondholders can be safely quartered in other, more lucrative positions earned by their past performances.

The third reason bonds today often resemble debt futures more than traditional debt obligations is related to the second reason. There is not only good money to be made buying riskier, higher yielding bonds but there also is a lot of money to be made packaging almost any form of debt in a bond format.

With so much money floating around seeking long-term relatively inactive havens, lest its sheer bulk be reflected in near-term inflation rates, anyone who can bundle virtually any sort of debt into a bond package stands to make out well. Even miniscule percentage commissions on large enough batches of OPM (other people's money) can add up to huge personal salaries and bonuses for bond packagers-peddlers.

In tandem, these factors have created a fair number of what one might term "new market mechanism risks" for bond owners (i.e., for *real* owners, not for their representatives or for the people who sell bond issues to these representatives) that are way out of proportion to possible rewards.

In the last year or two, these market mechanism risks have been accompanied by a number of problems related to specific bond marketplaces, which have added to the woes of bond investors. These difficulties came together in the first quarter of 1989 to produce average total returns on fixed income (bond) mutual funds of a paltry 1.2 percent.

The Environment's Role

How does the environmental factor fit into these present-day realities of bond investing? Mostly as a secondary factor in overall decisions about which bond issues or bond mutual funds to buy

Consider in this regard the different types of bonds and the kinds of environmental exposure their purchasers may face in years to come. The environmental factor has widely different applications and importance for treasury and government-backed issues, foreign bonds, tax-exempt (municipal) bonds, corporate bonds and mortgage-backed securities.

Treasury and government-backed bonds (like those issued by the Government National Mortgage Corporation—Ginnie Mae) are as free from environment-related default risk as they are from every other default risk. This is because if worst comes to worst (as it sometimes does), the same government that prints a currency accepted in debt settlement around the world can run the printing presses a bit longer to meet its own interest payment obligations. There are myriad other quasi-official obligations—from loans to farmers to loans to students to bail-out payments aimed at salvaging the savings and loan industry—that are not formally backed by the full faith and credit of the U.S. Treasury, but for all practical purposes, they are just as secure. Official backing of such securities has been strongly implied for so many years that failure to deliver in an emergency would undermine all federal debt obligations.

The only real risk for government bond holders is the inflation risk. The value of all fixed securities goes down when inflation increases. Thus, except in a very nebulous and distant manner, the environmental factor is not all that important in assessing whether or not to buy treasury bonds and other federally backed paper.

The situation is rather different when one looks at other sectors of the bond market. Many bonds issued by foreign governments *could* take a serious hit because of environmental deterioration or other negative environmental developments within countries where they are issued.

This is true about places like Poland, one of the West's biggest debtors and also a creeping environmental dead zone. It is true about Mexico, plagued by dangerous smog in its capital and chief financial center and by toxic-waste disasters-in-the-making in its currently booming northern tier. It is certainly true about Brazil, where the progressive destruction of the Amazon rain forest is a classic study of how advanced environmental decline can compromise the long-term debt repayment potential of a nation so economically active otherwise that it ranks as the world's eighth greatest industrial power.

To meet its current, already huge annual interest bill to foreign creditors, Brazil is expanding in ways that destroy a natural resource important to the entire world. To meet its long-term obligations to foreign creditors, Brazil is being asked not to destroy this resource, but to pursue a path of "sustainable growth."

Double-talk by international bankers and finance ministers, mixed with nationalistic bombast and Third World angst about not being able to destroy the environment with the same disregard for consequences once felt by Americans and West Europeans, occasionally obscures the linkage between a nation's environmental decline and its creditworthiness. But not for long.

The link is real and possibly critical to certain bond investors. People with holdings in large banks and other institutions that own the bonds of nations facing serious environmental crises should look carefully at the added risk to their capital represented by this particular manifestation of the environmental factor.

The Junk Flows In

The corporate bond market is currently littered with what even its issuers and sellers call "junk." Junk bonds are securities that bond-rating services categorize as less than investment grade.

Most of these low-rated issues now come from companies that have raised money not to buy new plant or equipment but simply to pay for the transfer of ownership from one set of managers to another set, or from one set of managers to a corporate raider. Common sense would seem to make such bonds suspect. Nonetheless, they sell like hotcakes because, until default, junk issues pay above-average interest rates, and thereby recommend themselves to institutions run by managers with short-term orientations.

Many junk bonds are questionable investments. It goes without saying that any serious economic downturn will almost immediately cause large numbers of defaults in the corporate junk bond field. And junk bonds issued by major polluters are always to be avoided. Any company that is overburdened with debt and is also prone to being hit with big environmental fines or judgments labors under a massive burden; such a company is especially susceptible to default.

The value of even investment-grade corporate bonds can be endangered by a serious environmental incident. Any petrochemical or utility giant faced with the threat of a huge settlement for environmental claims will likely see its bonds affected.

How many investors in today's bond market are at risk from this danger? *The Wall Street Journal* has a daily Bond Market Data Bank section. Under industrial bonds, it reports quotes for Amoco, Capital Cities, DuPont, Exxon Shipping, Eastman Kodak and Mobil. These bonds are selected because they are deemed representative samples of the entire taxable (i.e., corporate) bond market.

Four of these six issues are from oil or oil-affiliated companies with enormous potential environmental exposure. DuPont is a huge chemical firm that until recently was the world's largest producer of ozone-destroying CFCs. Eastman Kodak, not so long ago, offered to purchase property near one of its New York State facilities because of homeowner fears that pollution in the region might lower property values.

How immediate is the bond risk here? Shortly after the Valdez tanker incident *The Wall Street Journal* ran this headline: "Huge Oil Spill Spills Over into Sale of Exxon Notes."

Five utility bond issues are listed in another part of the *Journal's* Bond Market Data Bank. Each of the companies issuing these securities has nuclear or coal-fired facilities with environment-destroying propensities and, hence, with the environment-related potential to sour its bond ratings.

In today's securities markets, the indirect relationship between an environmental incident that causes a steep dip in a company's stock price and a crossover fall in the value of its bonds cannot be ignored either. A domestic Bhopal-like disaster, for example, could well send share prices low enough to attract corporate raiders.

If successful, such a raid would be financed by junk bonds, which would burden a company with new debt in such a way as to reduce the value of its already outstanding bond issues. If unsuccessful, the corporate defense used to fight off the raiders would also be likely to burden the company with new debt that would reduce the value of outstanding issues. Either way, environmental disasters could hurt bondholders.

The lessons here for bond investors are clear. At least be aware that issues from corporations with serious environmental exposure bear extra risks. Even investment-grade bonds could be at risk.

A parallel situation exists in municipal bond markets. Here, too, both junk and investment-grade issues could be endangered by environmental problems.

The $700 billion "muni" market was badly hurt by the 1986 Tax Reform Act. The measure eliminated special federal tax treatment of interest paid on certain bonds long favored by state and local governments. Without this form of federal subsidy, a goodly number of municipal bond issues were no longer marketable.

One major environmental consequence of this change is that as many as one-quarter of the communities in this country (most of them small towns with populations of less than 2,500) will now have trouble meeting tougher federal water and solid-waste standards because they can no longer raise money for new treatment facilities through bond issues. This was one environmental Catch-22 for the municipal bond market that resulted from tax reform. There are others.

More Junk

Just as there are junk corporate bonds, there are junk municipal bonds, rated at below investment grade. Some $24 billion worth of these securities were issued in 1988, a 55-percent increase from the year before. The largest number were issued by communities in Pennsylvania, with California and New York close behind.

In the wake of the 1986 Tax Reform Act, communities that could no longer find markets for their tax-backed and full-faith-and-credit-backed paper because buyers no longer found it attractive to buy such bonds without federal tax incentives as part of the deal began pumping out junk paper, often backed only by revenues from projects not even built yet (hospitals, bridges, etc.).

Could a junk muni's dividends be endangered by environmental problems? Of course. "Red-bag" waste is the sort of material hospitals generate by the ton. It is the used hypodermic needles, the bloody bandages, the test tubes filled with bodily fluids that wash up on beaches, as they did on New Jersey beaches in the summer of 1988. A serious red-bag lawsuit might cause the default of a junk muni whose backing is the revenue from the hospital that generates the offending waste.

Just as healthy corporate bond issues can be endangered in certain circumstances by some variant of the environmental factor, so can healthy (i.e., investment-grade) muni bond issues. In the early 1980s, the value of New York City's debt suffered because of the cumulative effects of overly generous past wage settlements with municipal unions.

Is it far-fetched to think that sometime in the next few years, a major city that is currently meeting all its bond obligations will have trouble doing so because of financial woes associated with disposing of its solid waste? disposing of its sewer sludge? complying with court or federally mandated environmental rulings?

The same approach we advised in our chapter on "The Environmental Factor and Stocks" applies to protecting the portion of an individual's capital invested in bonds. Check your personal bond portfolio. Carefully weigh the new risk that environmental exposure adds to each bond. If this tips the balance between acceptable and unacceptable risk-reward, sell the bond.

A Different Approach

Because most people do not own bonds directly, but indirectly through investments in one of the hundreds of bond mutual funds now in the market, a slightly different approach is needed to employ the environmental factor than is appropriate with stocks. It is difficult for the average fund investor to gauge the environmental exposure of the dozens of separate issues noted in the back of a typical bond fund's annual report.

An easier way to pursue this end is to simply call the fund and speak with its portfolio manager—or whoever takes the manager's calls. The basic question you need answered is what steps are used by the fund to protect investors from untoward environmental risks.

If the fund manager or spokesman does not seem to understand that municipal bond issues can be imperiled by environment-related problems of the sort that befell WPPS bonds, or that certain corporate junk bonds may have environmental-economic risks as well as the more conventional variety, it may be time to move one's capital elsewhere.

This is not ethical investing. It is common sense. If this particular variant of common sense happens to work in ways that favor prudent environmental activities, all the better.

CHAPTER 8

The Environmental
Factor and Commodities

Trading commodities has never been an activity for the faint-hearted. Commodity exchanges are one of the world's most blatant expressions of economic Darwinism. Energy levels here are high, and so, too, is an undisguised and unabashed willingness to piggyback profit on whatever circumstances, good or bad, happen to prevail in the world at any given time.

The environmental factor, as defined in this book, is starting to be appreciated in real estate circles. It is just beginning to influence thinking among stock buyers and sellers. It is still hardly considered at all in bond markets. In a slightly different guise, however, it is old hat in the commodities community. It is being picked up easily by traders here because it dovetails so nicely with one of the traditional predilections of commodities traders—an obsession with the catastrophic.

Commodity markets have always resonated to disaster. The threat or reality of war, revolution, trade disruptions, assassinations and other man-made tribulations has long influenced commodity prices strongly. Natural disasters such as floods and earthquakes are another underlying cause of many of the great jumps and dumps in commodity price history.

Another Disaster to Consider

The environmental factor can thus be viewed by commodity traders as just another variety of catastrophe. It has more importance in this market today for the simple reason that disasters directly or indirectly related to environmental decline are more common today than in years past.

Weather, for example, has always been the key to agricultural commodity prices. Freak weather patterns, caused in whole or in part by pollution-created conditions, suggest the growing influence of the environmentalist factor in shaping current agricultural commodity prices.

Natural upheavals such as earthquakes have caused precious metals prices to oscillate in years gone by. Unnatural upheavals, e.g., nuclear accidents or massive oil spills from leaking tanker hulls or bomb-ruptured drilling platforms, illustrate how the environmental factor is now producing the same type of oscillation.

When it comes to commodities, however, one must clearly distinguish between short-term symptoms of environmental decline and long-term symptoms. The former will become ever more important in influencing commodity price movements. The latter has almost no relevance in shaping commodity prices.

In a greenhouse-effect study released in late 1988, the EPA made the first major government predictions concerning how a warmer world might change the way Americans live. Among its conclusions was that decreased water runoff from the Sierra Nevada into California's enormously productive Central Valley will mean reduced production of fruits and vegetables; hotter summers will require more power plants to cool homes and offices; some coastal cities may someday find themselves under water as icecaps melt.

All these predictions, of course, have enormous economic implications. But none has any relevance at all to commodities trading.

In other doom and gloom environment-related scenarios, the Worldwatch Institute in Washington warned that human population increases are directly linked to unprecedented destruction of other species; U.S. scientists discovered that the ozone shield in various parts of the world is dissolving rapidly; Senator Albert Gore, Jr., in a *New York Times* Op Ed Page piece, warned of an impending "Environmental Ecological Kristallnacht."

None of these things has any relevance to commodities trading either.

Beyond U.S. borders, other agencies are reaching their own apolcalyptic-grade conclusions about how environmental decline is increasingly likely to provoke disasters affecting world grain and produce supplies. A few months after the EPA's greenhouse-effect study was released, the Economic and Social Commission for Asia and the Pacific, headquartered in Bangkok, predicted that devastating floods in Pakistan and Bangladesh and droughts in China, all caused by poor national environmental practices, would boost the number of food-reducing "natural" disasters in the 1990s.

These tragedies, too, are irrelevant in commodity trading. This is true because the time frame important to commodity traders runs only a few days to a few months. Contracts are all short-term. The bets in this market are on next fall's harvest or on the demand for gasoline during next summer's driving season.

The Effect Spreads

With increasing frequency, however, serious short-term manifestations of the environmental factor do occur in ways that affect commodity prices. And, as often as not, they not only affect prices of one commodity but also cause price swings in several others simultaneously.

Consider how the price of gold rose in the wake of Chernobyl because traders thought the accident might heighten tensions between the Big Powers. The price of grain futures rose concurrently because traders thought Chernobyl would lead to heightened Soviet demand for U.S. wheat.

In the same way, all sorts of metal prices, grain prices and currency future prices might be affected by environmental disasters. Consider the following environmental scenarios: A major earthquake in Japan or on the American West Coast causes either a nuclear plant or some large petrochemical facility to spew debris over a wide area. A devastating environmental leak or chemical spill in a Third World country with a huge foreign debt suddenly destroys its ability to maintain debt payments and threatens the international banking system.

Or consider these political scenarios with environmental overtones: A Middle Eastern country triggers a war when it attempts to monopolize water rights at a time when a neighboring country's own supplies are tainted by man-made wastes. The fear of a massive environmental disruption in Central Europe sets masses of people fleeing toward a border that the authorities decide to keep closed.

At the juncture where environmental decline meets the high-strung and generally dour world view of commodity traders, the effects of the environmental factor are strongly felt. Such is the nature of the commodity-trading beast.

Bond traders, after all, are natural believers in order and stability. How else could they possibly invest in instruments whose value depends on inflation remaining relatively stable for a decade or two? Commodity traders, on the other hand, live for sudden and nasty changes. They understand the environmental factor in their gut. In a twisted sort of way, it validates their professional lives. They do not shrink from the environmental factor, as do many other investors—people with so many other "factors" to consider that the thought of yet another seems intolerable.

In this way the environmental factor has achieved immediate and universal respectability among commodity traders. Droughts in the American Midwest, floods or monsoon failures on the Indian subcontinent, massive oil spills, crop failures in the Soviet Union—they are all related to man-made damage to the environment to a greater or lesser extent, and they are a growing source of inspiration for professional commodity traders.

The Hedge

Beyond trading, there is another use the environmental factor could have when it comes to buying and selling commodity contracts—hedging. Various commodity instruments are currently used as hedges by professional investors to protect them from untoward happenings of all kinds. Buying "environmental commodity hedges" could provide a kind of short-term insurance against the kind of slide in value many assets might suffer in the wake of environment-related mishaps.

Generally speaking, the environmental factor should weigh heavily for someone undecided about whether to take the optimistic or the pessimistic side of almost any commodity play. By our reckoning, all other things being equal, the pessimistic side is the way to bet. In today's world, there are so many possible large-scale environmental disasters just waiting to happen that the odds of one taking place during the life of a typical commodity contract get better all the time. To use a casino analogy, the environmental factor might be assigned the role of the house advantage—the little odds enhancer that over the long haul almost always turns a winner.

There is a ghoulish element to any discussion about environmental deterioration and commodity trading. Unlike the other good investing and good business techniques we suggest in this book, which foster personal profit while also working to improve the general health of the environment, there is no social utility in betting the bear on environmental decline through commodity investing. It is a money play, pure and simple.

If one can live with this tawdry reality, however (and experience suggests many commodity players can do so easily), the environmental factor, as an increasingly important variant of the catastrophic factor, may be regarded as a new fundamental in commodity markets.

It already animates commodity pits to a striking degree. This will become ever more apparent in years to come.

PART III

The Environmental Factor and the Workplace

CHAPTER 9

The Environmental
Factor and Executive
Planning

The environmental factor is not just useful to individual investors. It has (or should have) an important place in the thinking of every business executive.

In earlier chapters we saw how virtually every sector of the American economy is being buffeted by environmental decline and government efforts to cope with its consequences. Within certain industries, it is impossible to go to a convention, or even to a business lunch, without encountering some aspect of the environment-economy relationship.

A lawyer tells her business client that plans for expansion are being held up waiting for an environmental impact study. A production manager tells his foreman that there may be a shutdown because of new EPA standards concerning a certain manufacturing component that happens to be made of toxic materials. The maintenance department is trying to figure out safe ways to dispose of incinerator ash. These are all part and parcel of doing business today in the United States.

What is missing from the average executives' perceptions of environmental deterioration and its economic spinoffs is not a lack of daily exposure to the problems involved but a *perspective* from which to seek their solutions. In almost every plant and office, the environment-business nexus is still addressed in a piece-meal, often desultory manner.

Compliance by Convenience

The attitude is often, "Leave it to the company compliance person." It is an attitude that treats the environmental factor in business as if it is just another nuisance that can be sloughed off on middle management, the legal department or an occasional outside consultant, then quickly forgotten.

In many respects, this attitude among businesspeople is akin to the current attitudes among Wall Streeters when it comes to the environmental factor. Just as professional investors still tend to think about a few score common stocks when the economic implications of environmental decline are mentioned, many business executives still think only of complying with a few government regulations when the same subject arises.

We have already looked at some of the specific implications of the environmental factor for a dozen industries, such as banking, insurance, utilities and transportation. In this chapter, we focus on more general steps that can be taken by executives in small to medium-sized firms in virtually any industry, to lessen their present and future environmental exposure and, perhaps, even turn a bit of extra profit for their companies.

Consciousness-Raising

The first step to be taken in this field is to make all managers aware of the importance of environmental considerations in a company's overall business. Good managers are already quality-conscious. They are cost-conscious.

They are tax-conscious. They are conscious of the need for good employer-employee relations.

Environmental consciousness as it applies to company operations is just an extension of this approach. It is another basic measure of overall management skills.

The realms in which the environmental factor touch a company most directly should be emphasized in this consciousness-raising, of course. But so, too, should less obvious areas that are easy to overlook unless one has been properly "sensitized."

If your business involves manufacturing, for example, you already are aware of regulations related to discharge and disposal of industrial wastes. If it involves trucking, you know about rules pertaining to in-transit polluting. EPA rules requiring producers of toxic waste to inform local communities of possible dangers have awakened many companies to environmental risks. Expanded OSHA rules that require that hundreds of workplace toxics be tracked have had the same effect at other firms.

The difference between an executive who is merely irritated by these fast-changing requirements and one who is fully alert to their implications comes down to what might be termed "depth of vision." The merely irritated executive reacts to every new law, every tightened bureaucratic regulation, every damaging court decision, every market spasm reflecting the public's demand for more environmental responsiveness as something to be handled with minimum effort and expense. The fully alert executive is always planning ways to reduce negative company environmental exposure and even to benefit from them.

The merely irritated executive is a coper who is constantly surprised and embarrassed by the tightening environmental screw. The fully alert executive moves the company out of the way of environmental harm before unpleasant economic consequences can materialize.

From an ethical perspective, irritated executives might be viewed as classic polluters trying to avoid the hook as long as possible. But ethics aside, these persons are as much a profit menace today as a public relations embarrassment. Their failure to appreciate the changed importance of environmental considerations to a company's total operations is likely to be as damaging as a failure to recognize the importance of computer-generated business data in the 1970s would have been to successful business operations in the 1980s.

Once having recognized the importance of the environmental factor to a business, what specific steps can a manager take to meet its challenges? The first is probably to do the same thing we advised investors to do in earlier chapters—audit one's field of responsibilities.

Check the environmental hazards to which members of your work force are currently exposed and take steps to reduce their risks. Employee morale tends to improve when management is perceived as being concerned about such matters. As the lengthy and monumentally expensive litigation over asbestos exposure demonstrated some years back, failure to act aggressively can have devastating long-term economic consequences.

In defining and responding to workplace environmental hazards, it is usually wise to take a demanding attitude toward what is and what is not "hazardous." It has become painfully obvious to compliance professionals in recent years that when the EPA or some other federal or state agency changes environment standards, the change almost always *lowers* permitted thresholds of exposure. This being so, long-term programs based on techniques or processes that are barely acceptable today are likely to end up being completely unacceptable in years to come.

When doing environmental safety audits of a work force, executives should remember that paying someone else to cart away wastes or check for risks does not necessarily relieve the hiring company of future environmental liabilities. Managers must still closely monitor toxics and pollutants in their own areas of responsibility. Possible consequences of failure to perform this function include lawsuits and higher retirement health costs (paying for environment-related maladies) for offending companies.

The Buck Stops Here

Sometimes these consequences fall directly on derelict executives as well as on their companies. Individual executive liability for pollution-related disabilities is still in the legal nursery. Early indications, however, hint it may soon hit large numbers of individual executives quite hard.

Environmental audits with an eye toward protecting employee health are thus a prudent personal, as well as a prudent professional, step to be considered by today's corporate managers. Such audits also have special relevance when it comes to protecting the most important part of many a company's book value—commercial and industrial real estate holdings.

We looked at some general threats to this asset in our chapter on "The Environmental Factor and Real Estate." Here we focus on more specific risks.

The classic study of environmental deterioration and its effect on industrial property values is probably New Jersey. According to a *New York Times* report, since passage of the state's Environmental Cleanup Responsibilities Act in 1983, private concerns have had to pay $125 million to clean up 500 tainted industrial sites and post another $500 million in bonds toward the cost of cleaning up 17,000 additional contaminated sites identified by state officials.

New Jersey is somewhat special because it is much more densely populated and highly industrialized than most other states. But the economic moral for industrial property owners everywhere, somewhere down the road, is the same. Managing and selling tainted industrial properties is becoming a losing proposition.

A similar moral can be drawn for owners and would-be owners of commercial properties. Many of the same risks we cited as threats to residential property values in an earlier chapter are present in this field, too—often in a surprisingly stark form.

In early 1989, for example, officials discovered that a library located in the basement of a seminary in suburban Philadelphia was contaminated with the highest levels of radon ever recorded in a nonresidential structure. This prompted an EPA spokesman in Washington to comment that though his agency had previously been focusing on residential radon exposure, "I personally am [now] going to suggest people measure their work places."

The implications for businesses that own (and even rent) commercial space is clear. The environmental factor is becoming a progressively more important part of your real estate reckoning.

Beyond mitigating environmental health risks and protecting real estate assets, environmental audits should cover the full spectrum of production, distribution and merchandising activities in which a company engages. The aim of this exercise is to prevent fines and penalties before they are actually assessed.

In our technologically rich society, corporate toxic waste as often as not is the result of someone's failure to seek out a cleaner way to make, ship or market the same product or service that the company already makes, ships or markets. A simple "no-cost" substitution of one process or technique for another can often save thousands (or even millions) of dollars in fines and penalties down the road— if a smart manager takes the time and trouble to seek a solution.

In terms of how managers can take that step in time that saves nine, there is perhaps no more important application of the environmental factor than preventing a company-spawned, large-scale environmental disaster. There are rules and procedures that can be implemented to prevent such tragedies as the one in Bhopal, whether the cause of the disaster is maintenance or sabotage. Such steps, in fact, are already followed by most large U.S. companies, which explains why none of the 17 incidents that have occurred in the United States since 1965, according to an EPA study (and that released more toxics than the Bhopal tragedy) has had the same devastating consequences. Small and medium-sized operations should work to develop similar procedures.

These procedures should include steps aimed at mitigating the potential dire environmental spinoffs of natural, as well as man-made, disasters. Anyone who thinks about the subject for a moment realizes that natural disasters are as expectable—if not quite as regular and (more-or-less) predictable—as the seasons or the weather. There are thousands of earthquakes in the United States each year, hundreds of tornados, scores of floods, at least one or two serious hurricanes.

The Earthquake Factor

Possible megajolts such as the long-awaited Great California Quake are far from being a danger only to the West Coast. Every single county in the United States has found it expedient to maintain its own seismatic files. U.S. Geological Survey records show that a big earthquake struck the Boston area in the mid-18th century; one of the most powerful earthquakes ever recorded in U.S. history shook the Mississippi River Valley in the early 19th century; another major quake left heavy life and property damage in its wake around Charleston, South Carolina, in the latter part of the 19th century.

There was a fairly serious quake in California in June 1983 that did millions of dollars worth of damage. A far milder, but also far more surprising, quake rippled down the East Coast from Canada to Philadelphia in November 1988.

The relationship between the ever-present threat of natural disaster and environmental tragedy is this: The latter can compound the former in mind-numbing ways.

When a massive earthquake struck Tokyo in 1923, more than half the buildings in the then largely wooden city were leveled by shock and accompanying fires. There was no collateral environmental damage worth noting, however, because Japan's industrialization was not very far advanced. Today, if the same magnitude earthquake struck, most buildings in and around Tokyo would survive the shock because of stone and steel construction. But because the city is ringed by petrochemical complexes, the environmental consequences of such a quake are incalculable.

The 1988 Armenian earthquake cost 50,000 lives and an estimated $16.2 billion in property damages. Had there been a Chernobyl-like facility in the area, one cannot even speculate on what carnage might have resulted.

Corporate executives cannot stop the movement of the earth, cap volcanos or hold back hurricanes. They can, however, while doing environmental audits of their company's facilities, keep in mind that these facilities may one day be subjected to unusual natural stresses and must, therefore, be ordered in ways that make secondary environmental disasters less likely.

For petrochemical manufacturers, such prophylactic measures could be complex and costly undertakings. For managers in less environmentally sensitive enterprises, they might be nothing more than making sure a toxic-waste tank sits on mountings that "give" a bit should the earth shake, or that toxic-waste containers waiting to be hauled away are stored where a fresh tornado touchdown cannot release their contents. This sort of approach is square-one consciousness for the environmental manager.

The Bright Side

Not every use of the environmental factor by alert managers is preventive. In many instances, intelligent focus on environmental trends can generate additional corporate profits.

The first thing that comes to mind in this regard is a company's handling of wastes that have a scrap or recycling value. Most firms generate at least some materials that fit into this category. But most still do not take full advantage of the income opportunities.

Consider the paper on cardboard wastes that are the most common industrial and commercial recyclable. As noted in an earlier chapter, at the time of this writing the market for used paper and cardboard is soft, with supplies far outstripping demand. Present generators of paper and cardboard wastes must often pay to have this material taken away.

Supply and demand in this field, however, can turn around very quickly. When this happens, will the firm that now removes a company's waste paper and cardboard automatically cut its rates or voluntarily offer to pay for its feedstock? Of course not. Not unless an executive in the generating firm is actively and aggressively monitoring changing market prices.

The notion of in-house corporate paper recycling is very far from being an imaginative flight of fancy. AT&T has been very successful with just such a program in its Bedminster, New Jersey, headquarters.

A *Philadelphia Inquirer* story describes how the company made $372,000 in 1988 recycling computer printouts, envelopes, memos and magazines. The same story notes that had this paper not been recycled, it would have occupied more than 16,000 cubic yards in local landfills already overburdened with waste.

Companies such as AT&T, the Bank of America, MCI Communications and other large corporate paper generators now collectively recycle an estimated 200,000 tons of paper a year. The basic economics behind this approach is simple: in a state like New Jersey, where landfill space is disappearing, trash that cost $5 a ton to dispose of in 1970 now costs $100 a ton to haul away.

The most significant thing in the *Inquirer* article from our perspective, however, is the effect of this program on corporate image and employee morale. The former was so enhanced that the New Jersey Department of Environmental Protection issued a commendation to the company. Employees taking part in this environmental effort like it so much they occasionally stay late to help make it run smoothly.

Whether a company's "wastes" are paper or metals or rubber or solvents or plastics, there will likely be a way and a time when these materials can somehow contribute to the bottom line. But only if management is on its toes.

Packaging is yet another area where intelligent corporate appreciation of the environmental factor can produce excellent results. In terms of contributing to the national pool of solid waste, excess packaging has long been a prime villain. In terms of contributing to wider sales and company profits, the marketing potential of exploiting the environmental factor through control of packaging is still unrealized.

A great many consumers of all kinds of goods are now on the lookout for easy ways to "help the environment." Slimmed-down packaging bearing the message that it *is* slimmed-down packaging, perhaps tied in with the company's equivalent of a save-the-whale message, could boost sales at the same time it cuts packaging costs.

The entire area of environmental advocacy as a means of generating good will for companies and boosting their sales is just starting to percolate. In the past, this approach was largely used by petrochemical and insurance giants, who sponsored a few glitzy nature specials on television. Now, imagination is entering the field and the concept is spreading.

In the wake of bad publicity about pesticide-tainted fruits and vegetables, a major supermarket chain in eastern Pennsylvania took out full-page newspaper ads that not only boasted of its own efforts to promote "food safety" but also contained coupons demanding better government food inspection practices that reader-shoppers could clip and send their senators and congressmen. This is a good example of New Wave environment-conscious advertising.

Environmental Marketing

Before long we can expect to see sharp marketing managers not only "environmentally wrapping" their wares and decorating them with environmental messages, the way pictures of lost children grace the cartons of community-conscious food-sellers, but perhaps using packaging that bears the "seal of approval" of some local or national environmental groups as well. If the ABC Company has taken the time and effort to detoxify its production line and recycle its wastes and package responsibly, there is no reason this fact should not be recognized formally by some environmental group—for a fee.

Environmental activists need money. Companies need endorsements from popular individuals or groups. This is how the American Olympic effort is funded. Why should sharp promotional executives not take the same approach to the environment to sell their company's products?

"Internal" environmental promotions can also be profitably used to improve employee morale. Since so many people are favorably disposed to environmental protection these days, a company that does nothing more than put different receptacles in its cafeteria for solid waste (paper) and metals (aluminum soda cans) is making a cheap and easy statement of its community spirit.

If the idea seems to appeal to employees, it can be expanded to providing larger receptacles in the company's parking lot in which different colored glass, cans, cardboard or whatever are collected. In straightforward monetary terms, this sort of thing is a loss-leader. But then, so were company-sponsored ride-sharing programs during the energy crisis years and United Way collections today, for that matter. There are simply things a firm does to proclaim it has "arrived" at the point where civic activities are part of its regular fixed overhead.

Siting the New Plant

One of the biggest, most important decisions an executive is called on to make involves choosing a new site for a company plant or office. An entire industry of relocation specialists has sprung up over the years to assist in-house personnel on a matter so critical that its economic ramifications for a company are often comparable to the economic ramifications for an individual of choosing a new house.

When making the where to locate or relocate decision, in-house planners and their outside consultants look at such things as the cost of real estate in various areas under consideration. They look for a place with an existing or easily trainable workforce. They look at the present tax situation and often push for special tax treatment from local governments. They check school systems to make certain employees' children can be suitably educated. They ponder the matter of whether sufficient cultural and recreational opportunities exist nearby. They scrutinize a region's transportation network to ensure needed airports and rail links are handy.

Yet, when it comes to the environmental factor, these same scrupulous planners are often remarkably inept and shortsighted. They still tend to view the environment as a quality-of-life issue.

Everyone, naturally, wants to be located near pure water and clean air. But if the numbers look right otherwise, the tendency is to overlook environmental shortcomings and settle for the best *economic* deal.

As we note frequently in this book, however, the best economic deal is becoming more and more synonymous with the best natural environment. It is the function of alert executives to point this out, thereby protecting their companies from the consequences of poor environmental siting.

Forgetting for the moment the economic disasters that would surely result from buying and setting up shop in contaminated properties, just consider how a failure to give the environmental factor its proper due in less consequential ways could hurt a company's interests over a period of time.

Suppose the presence of polluting firms in the area causes local water supplies to be tainted, as has happened scores of times around the country in recent years. How much will it cost to truck in drinking and washing water for company employees?

Suppose the town or county where the new company facility is located runs out of space to put its garbage, or a court ruling changes overnight the way this material must be handled. How much could this cost in additional local taxes or in additional fees to hire private haulers to take a company's trash longer distances from its point of origin?

If the state where one is setting up shop seems gratifyingly slack in its present attitudes toward a company's own current polluting policies, is it likely to be that way in the future? How quickly could a ballot referendum or a legislative proposal alter a company's environmental overhead dramatically?

Who are the present and likely future neighbors for a company's new facility? What guarantees are there that a nasty polluter might not move into the neighborhood and quite literally knock the props out from under property values, or force nearby firms to pick up a hefty share of the costs of its own bad environmental practices?

If ozone levels are very high in the area during summer, will part of a company's workforce be out more often on high-ozone days because of extra health problems? Is the new facility near one of those congested areas where actual traffic to and from the job might be brought to a halt by government order during a "pollution emergency"?

The organization developing a property that an executive's company may lease or buy may have done its best to insulate the property to keep down heating and cooling costs. But what has it done to keep down direct and indirect costs of sick-building syndrome? And are its policies in this regard ongoing, or do they stop after the lease is signed?

There are far too many possible site configurations and related environmental risks that could come with each to do more than hint at all the elements that might go into using the environmental factor at any given new company facility. The key point here is that unless management makes this particular factor a priority in its deliberations, the chances of economic loss are great indeed.

Market environmentalism is valid for corporate decision-making, just as it is for personal investing and buying the family house. It is dumb to reward with your company's money, people, developers or communities who have unduly polluted their share of the general environment.

Why buy someone else's environmental mistakes? Why buy the environmental risks and exposure someone else has generated? Why take the economic gaff for someone else's environmental disdain, carelessness or stupidity?

Today's most incisive corporate managers need not go to Sierra Club or Greenpeace meetings in the evenings to atone for polluting sins they committed on the job during the day. They can bring to their daily work a hard-headed knowledge of the economic costs of polluting—and be better managers in consequence.

CHAPTER 10

The Environmental Factor and Employment Opportunities

In the 1967 film *The Graduate,* a confused, college-aged Dustin Hoffman is pulled aside by a well-meaning friend of the family who whispers a single word in his ear, "Plastics." The older man is conveying to the younger one the secret of financial success in years to come. If this scene were reenacted today, he might well whisper "Environmental services."

One of the oddest notions in current circulation is that protecting and cleansing the natural environment is a financial auto-da-fé, and that entering the field is roughly akin to shaving one's head and stumbling about with a cracked begging bowl. Environment-protectors still bear the image of storefront activists who collect used Pepsi cans when not distributing leaflets printed on biodegradable paper. In terms of making a living, the word "environment" remains synonymous in the public mind with lava lamps and love beads.

Anyone who has read the earlier chapters of this book knows this is nonsense, of course. But it is still worth outlining in some detail just how big an employer the environmental cleanup business is today, and the extraordinary opportunities it offers people seeking lucrative careers for the future.

Unfortunately, much of the data in this field must be gathered obliquely because information from the government is lagging well behind the times. The Bureau of Labor Statistics is still using Standard Industrial Classifications (SICs) formulated in 1972. Not surprisingly, these do not reflect the environment-related employment revolution that has largely taken place since 1980.

There were no SIC listings at all in 1972 for either "environmental services" or "pollution control." As this book was being written in early 1989, the Bureau was just implementing its updated 1987 SIC Manual.

When completed, it will contain just two environmental services listings—"Pollution Testing—Except Automotive Emissions," and "Pollution Control Agencies—Government." Even together, these two will only hint at the full scope of contemporary environmental employment.

This scope must be inferred by looking elsewhere. In terms of government environmental jobs, for example, the EPA now employs more than 16,000 people, while other federal agencies employ perhaps the same number. Some 27,000 people work on environmental monitoring and control for state governments, and a like number are employed in town, county and city agencies.

Employment Possibilities

Government environmental employment encompasses a diverse collection of skills. These include policy analysts, planners, coordinators, fine collectors, litigators, public relations specialists, inspectors and all-purpose administrators, as well as engineering staff. Federal environmental engineers have a starting salary of less than $20,000 a year, but after five years on the job this rises to $40,000 per year, with $75,000-a-year salaries for top slots.

The Encyclopedia of Associations lists more than 500 organizations active in the environmental field. Many are voluntary and civic organizations with only a few paid staffers. Others, however, have substantial numbers of paid staffers and represent companies and nonprofit groups with their own large cadres of paid workers and executives.

A great many other organizations listed in *The Encyclopedia of Associations* under headings like "Engineering" or "Chemical" are, for all intents and purposes, players in the environmental services industry. How else can one characterize groups representing various chemical manufacturing associations or associations of consulting engineers?

Private sector environmental engineering is, in fact, a boom profession. In 1985, just 5,000 engineers were working on cleaning up hazardous-waste sites. According to estimates of the Congressional Office of Technology Assessment, more than 11,000 will be needed by 1990, and more than 22,000 by 1995.

There are between 8,000 and 10,000 recycling centers now operating in this country. Someone opens the doors of these centers. Someone else trucks away the materials they collect. This is environmental employment.

A hefty share of operations in the aluminum industry is not concerned with making virgin product but with reprocessing already manufactured metal. The same can be said about operations in the paper, glass and scores of other industries. These reprocessing activities are environmental employment.

There has been a scrap industry in this country for a long time. Typically, its image has been of scruffy individualists, sitting in disreputable trailers, flanked by exceptionally nasty canines of questionable breeding.

The recycling imperative may soon lead to the sort of consolidation of scrap that occurred some years ago in the solid-waste sector of the environmental services industry. Here, "Ma and Pa" trash collectors and haulers were gradually bought out by national firms, which evolved into solid-waste holding companies. A similar evolution in the scrap field would add bookkeeping, public relations and managerial elements to the business and increase employment proportionately.

If one wanted to stretch the definition of "employment" à la recycling a bit, it might be observed that more street people probably derive incomes from gathering and turning in bottles, cans and other recyclables than from any other source save begging. Stretching the definition still further, it might also be noted that stealing old aluminum siding and window frames for sale to scrap dealers currently ranks among this country's most popular nonviolent crimes.

Countering environmental crimes has also become a major new source of employment. In this regard, work on the docks checking imported fruits and vegetables for environmental contamination will likely be the vocation of many hundreds of people in decades to come. So, too, will be checking poultry and livestock—not only for the FDA but also for private retailers and consumers who want an extra feeling of security about their edibles at a time when budgetary constraints are forcing cutbacks in the number of government inspectors. One might describe this trend as the environmental kosherization of America.

The tightening relationship between the security industry and the environmental services industry is well-understood by professionals in both. A visit to a modern landfill quickly demonstrates the point. These sites are a far cry from the unsecured ugly acreage that served the function in years past, with its mounds of garbage and burning tires and circling gulls, surrounded by low link fencing with an unsecured drop bar for the front gate and a rotting sign beside the gate saying "Closed on Weekends."

A modern landfill is more like a military installation. Its owners take serious precautions to prevent dumping of the "wrong" wastes, things like supertoxics that are legally required to be handled elsewhere.

More and more people are getting jobs as landfill guards. A growing number also work to protect and transport "red bag" hospital waste. Protecting all sorts of places from all sorts of hazardous or just plain unaesthetic wastes is a boom industry that is generating boom employment.

There are literally thousands of environmental service testing, monitoring and remediation companies doing business in the United States today. Many, especially in the part of the industry that deals with asbestos, are still Ma and Pa ventures employing a dozen people or less. But two industry giants, Waste Management, Inc., and Browning-Ferris, Inc., employed more than 31,000 and 18,000 people, respectively, by the end of 1987. These numbers have increased considerably since then. (See the environmental services industry employment table in this chapter.)

Most environmental service firms rank between the very large and the very small when it comes to employment. At the end of 1987, for example, Gundle Environmental Systems, Inc., had 320 employees; Groundwater Technology had 607; Enviropact, Inc., had 175; Envirosafe Services, Inc., had 285. When the payrolls of all such firms are lumped together, they add up to more employment than that accounted for by the few industry giants.

The types of jobs offered by environmental service firms tend to be heavily weighted to the technical side of the business. They include laboratory analysts, asbestos consultants, chemists, scientific site evaluators, "response" managers, biologists, hydrologists and engineering specialists of all kinds. But they also include community relations professionals, librarians, pipe fitters, laborers, tank testers, sales and marketing personnel, traffic managers and litigation support workers.

Along with environmental services firms, an increasing number of manufacturers now make and sell environmental equipment. Some of this is used at toxic-waste sites, some in plants and construction sites to clean the air. There is a growing list of manufacturers that also produce items that expedite urban garbage collection and recycling efforts.

A New Growth Sector

In terms of employment, it is interesting to note that growth in demand for environmental tools and equipment is more and more frequently taking up manufacturing "slack" in industries whose main or traditional business is not going all that well. Thus, some makers of farm equipment are boosting yard-waste and composting divisions to compensate for soft tractor sales.

The United States boasts more than 500 large design and engineering firms, many with hundreds of employees. A fair percentage of the work done by these companies is now related to some form of environmental cleanup.

There are 750 functioning private trusts that purchase land and see that it is kept out of the development stream. Most have modest-size staffs, but the largest employs 800 persons. Together, they employ thousands of people.

Hundreds and hundreds of other private trusts and foundations are today turning their attention and efforts to the environment. This changed emphasis is generating many new employment opportunities in this field.

Table 10.1 An Environmental Employment Sampler

Name of Company	Main Environ. Business*	No. of Employees End of 1987	No. of Employees End of 1988	Percentage Change
The BHA Group	Air Pollution Control	380	344	−10%
The Brand Companies	Asbestos Abatement	322	447	+39%
Browning-Ferris Industries	Solid Waste Mgt.	18,200	20,000	+10%
Calgon Carbon Corporation	Air Pollution Control	775	1,200	+55%
Canonie Environ. Services Corp.	Hazardous Waste Mgt.	228	375	+65%
Chemical Waste Management	Hazardous Waste Mgt.	2,900	3,870	+33%
Clean Harbors, Inc.	Hazardous Waste Mgt.	700	1,240	+78%
Davis Water & Waste	Water Treatment	595	734	+24%
Geraghty & Miller	Water Treatment	441	635	+44%
Groundwater Technology, Inc.	Water Treatment	607	897	+47%
Gundle Environ. Systems	Landfill Liners	320	613	+91%
Riedel Environ. Technologies, Inc.	Hazardous Waste Mgt.	356	545	+53%
Rollins Environ. Services	Hazardous Waste Mgt.	750	977	+30%
Waste Management, Inc.	Solid Waste Mgt.	31,000	36,000	+16%
Roy F. Weston, Inc.	Hazardous Waste Mgt.	1,850	2,441	+32%
Zurn Industries	Water Treatment	3,638	3,450	− 6%

*Many environmental services companies have more than one specialty. We only list the most important one here.

One of the chief opportunities for full-time environmental employment is in the "compliance" field. Jobs in this specialty usually involve seeing that companies are up to date and in accord with proliferating rules from all levels of government.

There are, of course, many company employees, especially in smaller firms, who perform these same tests for only a few hours each workweek. In the employment sense, these people might be considered environmental part-timers.

Among the biggest employers of full-time compliance help are petroleum companies, which have an ongoing and increasing need for environmental engineers. Chemical companies need more and more compliance professionals as environmental compliance becomes ever more complicated. Heavy manufacturing concerns and utilities are strong competitors in the job market and are seeking the same sort of skills. So are pharmaceutical firms.

Insurance companies advertise for environmental claims adjusters. Hospitals advertise for medical-waste disposal specialists. Some outpatient medical practices, especially in areas where toxic-waste incidents have been serious, now have environmental psychologists on their staffs. Environmental public relations, on behalf of either activists seeking to clean the environment or polluters seeking to carry on business as usual, is a flourishing specialty.

People now make a living giving out trash and littering tickets the way they make a living giving out parking tickets. Other people are making money collecting pollution and littering ticket fines.

Educational Opportunities

Education is a rapidly expanding sector of the environmental services field. More than 700 colleges and universities offer programs related to the environment, in addition to the hundreds of engineering programs that approach the subject from the mechanical and chemical perspective.

The reason for this growth is that the environmental consciousness of America's students is already highly developed and expanding rapidly. In the introduction to his book, *The Great Divide,* Studs Terkel notes a northwestern college where a majority of students pledged "to take into account the...environmental consequences of any job opportunity I consider."

Yale has a program in environmental studies. The University of Michigan has a School of Natural Resources. The New Jersey Institute of Technology just opened a Hazardous Substance Research Center. The Wharton School has an environmental club. Antioch's New England Graduate School has an environmental studies department that publishes a specialty job periodical called *Environmental Opportunities.* The number of environmental studies majors at Bowdoin College doubled over the last three years.

Environmental education is not just a university prerogative either. There are environmental trade schools cropping up in all parts of the country, training people in skills such as asbestos abatement. You already find these institutions advertising on matchbooks.

When writers and artists are considered as a branch of the environmental educational mix, the number of jobs for "environmental educators" soars another notch. Many big-city newspapers now employ environmental reporters. Bookstores are awash with hardcover and softcover books about the natural kingdom. Videomakers are entering this field in considerable numbers, producing tapes on everything from saving the rhinos to instructing homeowners about how to check for radon in their basements.

In the fine arts, painters like Anselm Kiefer are exploring the implications of environmental decline with increasing intensity. In the cinematic arts, *China Syndrome* is a typical example of the burgeoning environmental doomsday movie genre. Bo Diddley is singing about pollution. A Cagney and Lacey episode involved a dumping coverup. Dr. Who lectures on the subject weekly. And *The Toxic Avenger*, the "first superhero from New Jersey," has made a minor splash in video stores—even outside New Jersey.

The environment is among the fastest growing topics now covered by one of this country's most dynamic industries—the conference and trade show industry. Hundreds and hundreds of events are scheduled annually for scientists, legal and real estate professionals, and people looking for better ways to sell environmental products and services. One can sign up to hear specialists discourse on such catchy technical themes as the "Determination of Chlorinated Dibenzo-p-Dioxins and Dibenzofurans in Pulp and Paper Samples" or the "Dissipation of Soil Selenium by Microbial Volatilization." One can also hear lawyers compare costs of environmental compliance versus litigation or salespeople describe growing opportunities to sell treated sludge to farmers. All the discoursers, the people that prepare event mailings and collect reservation fees, represent kinds of environmental employment.

In cataloging full-time environmental employment opportunities, specialized professionals in a host of other fields deserve mention. Only one or two percent of all the lawyers in this country may be environmental full-timers, but this still works out to more than 5,000 lawyers.

The few thousand environmental full-timers in the insurance, banking, publishing and other businesses are tiny parts of their own industries. Collectively, however, they make up a rather significant professional talent pool.

Part of this pool also consists of consultants who make a living providing environmental data to companies that cannot generate it in-house. The *World Environmental Directory* lists more than 3,000 such consultants in its 1989 edition.

What the Employment Numbers Mean

When you add them up, the number of people who could qualify as full-time environmental workers and professionals in this country today is probably several hundred thousand. And to this total can be added the even larger number who spend part of their working day on environmental cleanup projects.

This group includes socially conscious mutual fund managers who follow a few environmental service stocks, plumbers who check for asbestos pipe linings while fixing a leak, real estate lawyers who work on environmental clearances from time to time, and on and on.

Viewed from the perspective of the way the world really operates, instead of from within the narrow parameters established by Wall Street analysts and Bureau of Statistics number-crunchers, the environmental cleanup industry is actually one of the largest employers in the country. One might make an analogy here with the tax industry.

From the "official" point of view, the tax industry consists of 100,000 people working for the IRS, the additional thousands of tax employees with state and local governments, a few thousand lawyers and accountants, and some demiprofessionals who occupy storefronts between early February and mid-April. In fact, however, so many people spend so much of at least some of their business days working on tax matters, that tax compliance and tax avoidance are far and away the most significant economic activity in the country.

Environmental cleanup should be viewed in much the same light. It is now one of our most significant national economic activities. As such, it is, by definition, one of the country's largest employers.

Before passing on to entrepreneurial opportunities in the environmental field, one other important point should be made about vocational environmentalism. In a very real sense, it is an *unlimited* field of employment.

Over and above the hundreds of thousands of explicitly environmental full-time positions and the many other jobs that occasionally entail environmental cleanup functions, virtually any kind of work can be infused with positive environmental purpose from time to time. This is true whether one works in a factory or in an office. It is true whether one's job is janitorial or executive.

One of the things that makes religious life so appealing to so many people is that it allows the simplest actions to be filled with significance. Washing is raised to ritual. Sharing food and drink becomes a prayer. Wearing certain garments and performing certain rituals are overt means of expressing deep-felt feelings toward the universe.

The same sort of feelings can animate nonreligious people with strong personal philosophies. The ability to fill one's days with actions that are felt to be part of something important gives anyone's life a sharper edge.

For both the religious and nonreligious, a positive environmental stance at work is a splendid way to make the day more enjoyable. The simplest on-the-job recycling of office or plant waste substitutes a sense of "doing something" for a sense of helplessness in the face of growing pollution everywhere. It creates another subject of conversation for after business hours. It provides excellent outlets for on-the-job initiative.

People who use the environmental factor at work become more productive. The act of becoming more aware of the environmental consequences of a job makes one more aware of work surroundings generally. Awareness begets awareness, which, in turn, raises productivity.

Properly harnessed, the sense of participation and purpose the environmental factor provides in virtually any workplace could beneficially ripple through the entire economy.

CHAPTER 11

The Environmental Factor and Entrepreneurship

Not everyone who wants to earn a living helping to clean up the environment wants to work for someone else. Many Americans see starting their own businesses as the most satisfying and profitable way to participate in this endeavor.

There are so many manifestations of entrepreneurial environmentalism bubbling through the economy today that it would be impossible to catalog them all. They include a host of minienvironmental service operations that do everything from consulting with property owners about "sick-building syndrome" to aiding small firms with their environmental compliance paperwork.

They also include part-time positions of the sort increasingly favored by skilled tradesmen. One can now make a fair amount of money encapsulating asbestos around piping in the evenings and patching underground tanks on weekends.

One of the chief forces behind new environmental services entrepreneurial activity is something one might term "the quality-of-waste issue." Each year ecological systems become more overtaxed and their ability to handle additional human wastes diminishes. Each year scientists learn more and more about the long-term dangers associated with smaller and smaller amounts of waste.

One consequence of these trends is that calls go out for changes—tightenings—of existing environmental regulations. Sooner or later, these calls bring about responses from the authorities.

Sometimes, when environmental standards are tightened, a company already in the field expands or changes its operations to take over a newly created business. More often, a newcomer, an entrepreneur with a different technique or better equipment, moves in to take advantage of the new environmental opportunities and make the profits.

A curious aspect of this perfectly natural and healthy evolution is that it turns yesterday's environmentalists into today's polluters. The same people who fought for tighter standards in the late 1970s, so they might establish an enterprise, now frequently lead the fight against still higher standards because it represents a threat to their livelihoods.

Changing, tightening waste-quality standards create a constant need for new environmental entrepreneurs. And given the state of the overall environment, higher waste-quality standards are inevitable.

Along with environmental services, two other areas deserve special mention when it comes to illustrating the extraordinarily rich and diverse entrepreneurial opportunities being created by environmental decline and government attempts to check its spread. We briefly looked at both from an investor's perspective in an earlier chapter —environmental self-defense products and recycling.

Environmental Self-Defense

When the British were ruling India in the last century, one of the most common observations of the colonizers concerned Indians' "odd" notions of cleanliness. On the one hand, their public sanitation practices were appalling. Open sewers were everywhere and people often used the same water for bathing and drinking.

The personal hygienic practices of the Brahmin caste, however, were far more thorough than those of the occupying British. Brahmins spent more time during a day cleaning their teeth than the average Englishman spent cleaning his entire body.

In a sense, this same discrepancy between standards of public health and standards of private hygiene has become the norm in the United States of America at the end of the twentieth century. We wallow in the filth of a corrupted environment but take extraordinary steps to protect our own health through elaborate prophylactic measures and personal detoxification.

The environmentally sanitized house or office is as much a symbol of contemporary affluence and power as is the reserved parking space. The visual metaphor of our times is a tastefully sneakered and sweatbanded jogger fighting to achieve bodily perfection while loping through sickening banks of urban smog. The marketing buzzword for our times is "purity."

No group of entrepreneurs has picked up on this faster than marketers of environmental self-defense products. The first entrepreneurial products and services that come to mind here involve radon testing. A radon test kit is little more than some activated charcoal in a dehumidified canister. A radon testing service is a man or woman who can read the gauge on a device that measures gamma rays.

Some experts in the field believe that more than 100 million radon tests will be conducted in homes and buildings by laypeople and specialists over the next five years. To date, an estimated 1 million or so have been performed.

The present radon market is thus very tempting for those who favor self-employment. Its start-up capital requirements are modest. It has a huge untapped cus tomer potential. The technical end of the business is not especially onerous. Its service, and even its manufactured hardware, appeals to part-timers seeking second incomes.

Ultimately, of course, there will be a shakeout of kit-makers, with a large market share going to a few specialty independents and to plumbing supply firms that have bought up their competitors. The service end of the radon testing business will increasingly be dominated by plumbers and contractors as a sideline, rather than by specialists.

The same transition from environmental specialty to a standard component of the heating, ventilation and air-conditioning (HVAC) industry is likely with drinking water self-defense products. At present, you can buy test kits that identify the nasties coming out of the family faucet and a wide assortment of devices that actually filter or otherwise cleanse potables.

Prices range from $20 or so at the low end of this mar-ket to several hundred dollars for systems on the higher end. They are sold both at K-Marts and in the places where people once bought their Cuisinarts.

Given the deteriorating quality of drinking water in so many large cities where municipal piping is overaged and in smaller communities where local governments can no longer pay police and firemen, much less afford the costs of purifying their drinking water, demand for new self-defense products in this realm is certainly going to soar. Again, after established housewares manufacturers move in, the entrepreneurial winners will include a few surviv-ing independents.

When it comes to environmental self-defense products, the most successful small-business owners and entrepre-neurs will not always be in the most obvious "environmen-tal businesses." They may be people who simply add an environmental twist to their current marketing.

The Food We Eat

Americans are frightened about the food they eat, just as they are frightened about the water they drink. This fear is exploited nightly on television with commercials that not-so-subtly exalt the health-preserving qualities of various fibers, whole grains, nuts, fruits and berries.

Raising and selling organic fruits and vegetables, grown without pesticides, has been an entrepreneurial exercise for decades. It now involves thousands of farmers, packagers and health-food-store owners.

There was a leveling off in this industry during the early 1980s as the interests of the baby-boomer generation focused on making a buck. The prime buying public in this period was more interested in microwaving its meals so as to have more time in the office than in carefully shopping for healthful comestibles.

Today, eating safe is again a national priority, in large measure because of fears about pollution-tainted food. Entrepreneurial health-food producers and sellers who are successfully picturing their wares as a personal defense against environmental decline are doing very well indeed.

Though only an estimated one percent of the produce grown in this country is raised organically, this now represents a billion-dollar-a-year annual market, twice what it was just five years ago. Though attracting growers like Sunkist and Dole, it is still largely dominated by Ma and Pa entrepreneurs, and is likely to remain so in the future.

Organically grown fruits and vegetables have gotten very popular, very quickly. Prices for this produce are high. Demand exceeds supply. Profits are soaring for both growers and retailers.

Every well-publicized food scare boosts the trade. Though only about five percent of this country's apples are treated with Alar, cancer worries associated with this chemical caused an enormous drop in apple and apple juice purchases after stories about Alar hit the media in the winter of 1989.

Even if not directly related to environmental decline or chemical tainting, food scares of all kinds now work to raise people's consciousness about possible pollution of their food. When a few Chilean grapes were found to be laced with cyanide, the $800-million-plus Chilean winter fruit and vegetable industry (and its numerous American affiliates) were briefly threatened with disaster.

In the wake of this grape scare, *Organic Gardening Magazine* hired Lou Harris & Associates to do a survey on public attitudes toward organic produce. Forty-nine percent of those surveyed said they are now willing to buy it, even if it costs more. The entrepreneurial implications of these findings are obvious.

This is a field where imaginative marketing could generate impressive payoffs. "Organically grown" has long been a big selling point for fruits and nuts and vegetables. "Greenhouse grown" could have a similar positive impact on sales in years to come.

Already, in parts of California, where much of this country's fruits and vegetables are raised, cultivators are beginning to move their operations indoors under glass and plastics because outdoor air is so full of toxics. This tragic reality opens interesting new selling possibilities for health-food dealers looking for a catchy marketing hook.

In a similar vein, fear of toxics in food is leading to profits for those who ensure that there are none. A company in California now tests pesticide levels in fruits and vegetables. After they "pass" on products, supermarkets can note that fact in their advertising. At the time of this writing, the company's business was booming.

Another established industry that stands to experience a resurgence because of greater awareness of environmental decline is raising and selling nonedible plants and flowers. Garden trees and house plants have always been sold as objects of beauty. The era when they will also be marketed as air filters has arrived as well. In the not-too-distant future, plants that change color in response to unhealthy levels of certain pollutants may become as common in American households as purification devices on kitchen water taps and radon test kits on basement floors.

There is a whole new "environmental" edge emerging in home lawn care as well as in-home plant raising. Recent announcements, like one suggesting that 40 commonly used lawn products contain chemicals dangerous to human health, are leading people to use such nontoxic lawn helpers as insecticide soaps. Alternative in-home treatments that kill termites by pumping liquid nitrogen into walls instead of toxic fumes are another facet of the same trend. Opportunities in this market for entrepreneurs are proliferating rapidly.

The Clothes We Wear

The environmental self-defense marketing motif will find its way into all sorts of other product and service pitches in the 1990s. Certainly, many will involve clothing.

There already is a branch of the rag trade that profitably manufactures chemical protective clothing—a kind of apparel so specialized that it is typically marketed under the initials CPC. Just as AIDS boosted the demand for latex gloves among medical, dental and even security personnel who frequently encounter people who are bleeding, increasing exposure to nasty chemical pollutants is creating enormous new demands for CPC.

What makes this particular field so open-ended is that different fabrics and fibers are needed to protect people against different pollutants. Without in any way gloating about the fact, one might note that every time the toxicity rating of a hazardous-waste site is raised or acceptable health thresholds for various waste are lowered, new opportunities appear for clothing manufacturers.

Along with pragmatic shifts in work apparel, fashion in general is gradually accommodating new environmental realities. Hats, for example, are making a strong comeback. With the ozone shield wearing thin in so many places, how could it be otherwise? More people are also wearing ultra-violet rated, non-prescription sunglasses because of fears of eye damage from excess exposure to harmful solar radiation. "No exposure at the temple," reads one ad from a Tennessee hatmaker. "Plenty of shade for side of face and back of neck," the ad continues.

Look for generally more conservative swimwear in summers to come. Look for new transparent beach accessories that let one view limbs and such but that keep out dangerous solar radiations. Look for a surge in sales of portable beach cabanas where people can safely hide from the same tanning rays they used to seek so avidly.

Cosmo once told its readers to "think pink." If one were picking the fashion colors of the 1990s, thinking green and white might be good bets.

Environmental entrepreneurs will make and market quite a number of fashion items. In some cases, they will also sell these through franchised outlets. From a certain perspective, the large number of tanning franchises now operating around the country can be viewed as an early example of environmental franchising.

Along with fashion and health-and-beauty franchise opportunities, environmental franchises built around toxic-waste cleanup systems will become more popular. There is no reason to suppose environmental franchising of all kinds will not increase significantly in years to come.

Where We Live

Perhaps the ultimate in environmental self-defense "products" are the entire residential communities now being planned around the concept of providing environmentally sound living space. The movement was inspired, in part, by a 1975 novel called *Ecotopia*, which described how three West Coast states seceded from the Union and set up their own country run on principles that accorded with nature.

The few "ecotopic" communities now functioning around the country have a lot of open spaces, a lot of home-based professionals in residence, neat bike paths, lots of solar panels, organic gardens tended by locals, and buy-in prices that hint that environmental salvation at the community level might be an option strictly limited to the upper middle class. Naturally, with this kind of *cachet*, the concept is spreading like wildfire.

In early 1989, a group called the Maharishi Heaven on Earth Development Corp. was reported lining up builders near major cities to construct 50 "noise-free, pollution-free and stress-free communities" in neighborhoods throughout North America. These communities are to be built with nontoxic, natural materials. According to at least one developer considering taking part in the plan, the concept addresses homeowners' current prime anxiety—environmental problems.

It is perhaps more than coincidental that the idea for these communities had roots in thinking that originated on the Indian subcontinent. A traditional Brahmin quest for personal cleanliness and purity in the midst of communal filth and crowding finds almost cosmic expression in this sort of real estate venture.

Recycling

The most immediate entrepreneurial opportunities with respect to environmental preservation and restoration concern recycling. Recycling, in fact, probably offers the most important entrepreneurial opportunities of any sector of the entire U.S. economy.

What makes this activity so "real" today is that the myths and misconceptions surrounding it have finally begun to fade. People have come to realize and accept that recycling is usually quite labor intensive and hence not all that cheap to implement.

They have also come to appreciate that large-scale recycling involves more than voluntary efforts by a good-hearted citizenry. It generally requires some form of coercion to function successfully. Fining citizens for not segregating household trash and ticketing merchants who do not sweep in front of their shops are two such forms of coercion. They exemplify adult, late-1980's recycling reality, and are, by-in-large, being accepted as such by most Americans.

In an earlier chapter, some numbers were provided which suggest the overall growth of recycling in recent years, along with statistics relating to materials the public usually thinks of as "recyclable." To get a real flavor of the extent of emerging entrepreneurial opportunities in this field, however, one should look beyond the 1970 parameters, which focused exclusively on metals (e.g., aluminum), on rubber, on glass, on paper and on cardboard.

Today's much expanded recycling horizons include such things as corn husks, formerly left to rot in the fields. A biodegradable plastic is now made from this material, and it is being used extensively in shopping bags.

Common substances that accumulate in back yards are also being viewed less as wastes and more as resources. Fallen leaves and grass clippings presently account for about 17 percent of all municipal waste, and as much as 75 percent in autumn. Depending on where one lives, old leaves and grass can cost cities, individuals and businesses as much as $115 a ton to haul away to landfills.

The recycling answer to this old problem is composting, which converts leaves and grass into a natural fertilizer. A number of countries in Europe have long been active practitioners of this approach. In Sweden, according to *BioCycle Magazine*, about 25 percent solid waste is composted; in France, 5 percent; in West German towns (e.g., Heidelberg), about 33 percent.

Compost-Recycling

In the United States, compost-recycling is catching on quickly. Its success, in fact, is crucial to meeting the EPA's overall solid-waste reduction plans.

Composting programs are already cutting some landfill costs in New Jersey communities by more than 80 percent. Large-scale municipal composting programs are operating in scores of cities around the country, including Minneapolis, Minnesota; Madison, Wisconsin; Davis, California; and Seattle, Washington.

Profitable entrepreneurial opportunities in this domain include everything from hauling and equipment manufacture to publishing. Entrepreneurs with the skills and patience to deal with municipal officials can organize programs and sell equipment that cuts city solid-waste disposal expenses—and often make out handsomely in the process.

There are engineering firms now selling complete composting systems. Farm implement manufacturers are boosting their yard-waste accessory lines. Hundreds of compost consultants and planners are setting up shop and offering their services to both "producers" and unwilling "consumers" of yard wastes. New books on composting, many of them desk-top productions, are appearing all the time. There are a growing number of seminars and workshops on the subject.

All of these activities are somebody's business. All generate profits.

Another kind of compostable material is sludge. Sludge is sewage with some of the water removed. Laced with all kinds of industrial toxics and heavy metals, it is one of the greatest dangers to drinking water supplies and fishing grounds. Purified and dehydrated, however, it becomes a valuable fertilizer, an export that gets shipped to Taiwan for use in pipe manufacture or, at the very least, a waste that is much cheaper to get rid of.

New types of sludge-handling equipment are appearing almost daily. Sludge consultants, planners and systems salespeople are cropping up everywhere. Some companies now market mobile sludge units that will visit a company plant and turn impossible-to-dispose-of effluent into waste that local trash collectors will accept.

The need for new types of trash-handling equipment of all kinds is a bonanza for sharp entrepreneurs. Such equipment and techniques for employing it effectively dovetail perfectly with a primary need of the times.

The Seattle approach to solid-waste collection, which features standardized trash barrels the city picks up for a fixed fee per container, is what the future of American municipal waste handling is all about. Increasingly, people will be charged directly and individually for services such as trash collection once paid for indirectly with taxes.

In the realm of municipal solid wastes, this opens up splendid new chances for profit for businesses that help city administrations levy "user fee" exactions on their citizenry. A municipal trash container contract in years to come will be as much a cash cow for the company that has it as a contract to collect overdue parking fines is today for the lucky holder of a collection contract.

With respect to solid waste and recycling, one need not think big to make a buck. Recycling bags in all shapes and sizes are being marketed by many companies and sold to condo associations and building management firms.

Designer Garbage?

The tribulations of a Long Island garbage scow captain seeking a home for his vessel's contents generated a lot of national publicity not so many months ago. These tribulations spawned a new minibusiness as well. Some of the scow's contents are now being sold as "designer garbage."

Repackaging trash as objets d'art and transferring small units from landfills to coffee tables may not do much to solve this country's overall solid-waste problems. But at least it suggests that the entrepreneurial imagination is finally reaching critical mass in this field. In a similar novelty vein, you can now buy bottles of undiluted Boston Harbor water and rubber neckties made of discarded tires.

Hints about the ultimate potential for recycling many common forms of solid waste are to be found in the present success of recycling a material like aluminum. During the 1980s, more than 10 billion pounds of aluminum were recycled in this country. Most of this took the form of reprocessing beverage cans, but aluminum auto parts and assorted wrapping material were also recycled by the ton.

Perhaps the most significant thing about this extraordinary success was that it was exclusively a private, rather than a government-sponsored, venture. Recycling the metal requires just 5 percent of the energy necessary to make it from bauxite ore. This led the aluminum industry to appreciate the merits of recycling shortly after the 1973 energy crisis. Voluntary, economics-based industry action resulted in the kind of results that officially run or underwritten programs almost never achieve.

In general, government recycling efforts work best when they are "indirect" in nature—i.e., when they simply create conditions that make recycling a given material profitable or disposing of a material in inappropriate ways terribly costly. A few examples illustrate this point.

Solvent recycling is a profitable venture for some waste handlers today, not because government regulations directly require it but because regulations of some states make safe disposal of solvents so costly that companies will pay someone else to take the job off their hands. A solvent recycler can thus make money on the collecting as well as the resale end. Businesses that now successfully collect and reprocess waste lubricating oil grew in exactly the same way.

When it comes to rock aggregate, the land-use laws that govern how structures can be built in many cities have caused problems for firms that must unload a lot of stony material after demolishing a building. The result? Favorable economics for crushed-stone recyclers.

Another kind of indirect incentive to recyclers is found in the growing landfill crisis in places like the Northeast. Shortage of dumping sites in this region has led to many landfill operators refusing to accept old tires. The result? Increased incentives to develop new uses for this material, including using it as a base for new roadbeds.

Many other items clogging landfills are responding to this same new recycling imperative. Disposable diapers have been estimated to account for almost two percent of the total material buried in dump sites. The result? A new generation of disposable diapers that is less bulky and more biodegradable than its predecessors.

In looking at the overall need (and hence the overall potential) for recycling, it might also be noted that artificially enhancing processes once handled by nature unaided is becoming another economic growth area. As water resources become short in many parts of the country because of population growth or as a consequence of other forms of overdevelopment, the need to reduce pressures on sewerage systems that handle human waste grows. Manufacturers and retailers of short-flush toilets and totally organic no-flush models, along with makers of watersaving shower heads and the like, are benefiting accordingly.

The hottest market for recyclables now and into the foreseeable future is probably plastics of all kinds, discussed at some length in an earlier chapter. This is not just a field for companies the size of DuPont or Waste Management, but one where innovative small-scale entrepreneurs can also find a host of profitable niches.

Dozens of people reading these lines will become millionaires in the plastics recycling business during the coming decade. This personal financial growth is directly tied to enterprises that benefit the environment.

PART IV

The Environmental Factor and the Future

CHAPTER 12

The Environmental Factor and Economic Forecasting

Economists are fond of saying that theirs is not an exact science. Setting up macromodels of economic systems that may have thousands of variables is a tricky business. Trying to devise mathematical formulas that encompass the psychological quirks that are part of human buying and selling decisions is a challenge that can frustrate the best minds.

This explains, in large measure, the failure of most professional economists to factor environmental considerations into their forecasting. For years, a few people on the fringes of the economic establishment have been pointing out the potential economic consequences of environmental decline. But the difficulties in quantifying this decline in terms professionals could work into their computations and the sheer magnitude of other data that seemed to be more important in shaping near-term events caused such views to be largely ignored.

The reason this is changing so drastically today is not just because unpleasant new realities are suddenly emerging. Environmental problems were bad and getting worse in the Reagan years, too. That administration, however, had a strong popular mandate not to focus on bad news. With a new administration in Washington and a different mood taking hold in the country, news of environmental problems and their associated economic corollaries are turning up in the press with astonishing frequency.

The forecasting consequence of this turnabout is that conventional economists around Boston, Philadelphia and points west are being forced to take note of a trend they previously either ignored or downplayed. The notion that the man-made ecologies known as economies exist within larger ecologies known as environments is finally seeping into the economic dialectic. The idea that happenings in the broader sphere are reflected in the lesser sphere is beginning to be explored.

A new rhetoric and new sets of variables are being developed. In response to demands from their corporate and government clients, this nation's 100,000 professional economists are positioning themselves to capitalize on this "new" trend.

The Voice of the Press

What sort of headlines and news stories are causing this change in orientation among economic professionals and the people who employ them? One could use almost any newspaper on virtually any day to find examples. Because this book happens to be written in Philadelphia, and this chapter is being prepared in mid-March 1989, we use the March 18, 1989, edition of the *Philadelphia Inquirer* as a perfectly random sampling of how environmental decline and economic health are now inexorably linked.

This is a Saturday edition, usually the paper's smallest of the week. The day chosen had no monumental environmental disasters like Chernobyl, Bhopal or the Valdez oil spill dominating its headlines. And though the *Inquirer* dutifully covers environmental issues, it is certainly no barn-burner on the subject (the paper, for example, does not have a regular Environment section, as does *The New York Times*).

The stories cited below all came from the *Inquirer's* first section, and do not even include additional material from its Metro or Business sections. As a typical example of environment-economic news turning up in big-city dailies today, this material is thus not skewed to prove a point.

In a story headed "Inflation Worries Mount," the Labor Department's Producer Price Index for February was reported showing a one-percent wholesale price jump. A goodly share of this rise was represented by increases in the costs of food and energy. Both food and energy costs, as we demonstrate in earlier chapters, are responding to environmental degradation and pollution.

Another story in this edition of the *Inquirer* more directly points up the relationship between pollution and inflation. "FDA Lets in Fruit from Chile under Tighter Security," runs its three-line head. The article tells how fears about the safety of fruits and vegetables from Chile caused temporary ripples of unemployment among dock workers in the Port of Philadelphia and elsewhere.

A related story headed "Scramble to Find Fruit Forces Prices Upward" details the inflationary consequences that result when a pollution scare drives shoppers to seek "safe" food in a market where sellers can demand premium prices for their wares. While it should be emphasized again that this Chilean incident was not the result of agricultural contamination but of deliberate tampering, the inflationary implications are the same.

Directly under the "Scramble" story was a piece headed "Shipments of Apples Down." This chronicled the falloff of sales of Washington State apples in the wake of the Alar scare. This was an instance where human-made contamination clearly and directly produced an economic result.

Another headline in this day's *Inquirer* read, "Sweeping Anti-Smog Plan Approved." The story tells of a regional air quality plan in Southern California aimed at bringing the area into compliance with existing environmental laws and regulations. In the story, business and labor groups predicted the plan would cost thousands of jobs in the region. One critic of the plan was quoted as saying that "under this plan the government assumes complete regulatory control over people's lives."

Perhaps the paper's most obvious example of how the environment works on the economy was found in a front-page story headed "Here's How to Save the Environment." Discussing some possible economic affects of the greenhouse effect in the next century, an EPA official described a cornucopia of economic probabilities, ranging from more efficient cars to changes in the chemicals used by industry to the need for a different mix of fuels in electric power plants. Collectively, just to mitigate the effects of a single environmental challenge, the greenhouse-effect, the official outlined steps that, if implemented, would add up to an economic revolution that would make Marxism look like a change in bulk mail postal rates.

Dr. Dooley once noted that the Supreme Court may not always follow legal precedents but does always keep up with the election returns. Professional economists are equally inclined to follow the news that turns up with their morning coffee and croissants. As media coverage of environmentally linked economic decline intensifies, economists move naturally to expand their "coverage" of this field.

There are much more than professional protocols involved in this shift of attitude and emphasis. For individuals who employ the environmental factor, a much expanded focus by economists on matters environmental has considerable importance. It means that the value of personal investments and the worth of personal business decisions will be increasingly influenced by a market atmosphere where "the big boys"—the people who move around the most capital and hire the most prestigious economic consultants to help them do so—will be betting more and more on environmental decline.

In this sense, irrespective of whether it truly represents the state of things in the world today, the environmental factor may be viewed as a self-fulfilling economic prophecy. Individuals who buy into this prophecy early enough will, therefore, have a financial leg-up when a more general, expert-inspired awareness of the relationship between environmental decline and the general economy begins to affect operations in every sector of the marketplace.

CHAPTER 13

Who Will Pay the Environmental Tab?

The environmental factor has immense personal value to investors, executives, people seeking career opportunities and entrepreneurs. To fully appreciate its importance to society as a whole, however, one must confront the fact that there is no mechanism other than the individual-based environmental factor that offers the slightest hope of satisfactorily resolving this nation's current crop of environmental problems.

We briefly touched on the inadequacy of government resources in this realm in earlier chapters. We noted some of the extraordinary costs of remedying past pollution and contamination damage. Looking more closely at these costs, at the full extent of environmental deterioration and the capital available to make it right, it immediately becomes clear that the balance is askew.

Government and business together come up short when it comes to paying the bill to keep this country fit for human habitation. They come up short even if one works into the equation a sharp temporary decline in national living standards, with capital removed from the consumption pool and directed into environmental retooling instead.

The only surplus that could conceivably fill this gap is the individual activities of millions of Americans applying the environmental factor. What the ordinary functioning of our political and economic institutions can no longer achieve in coming to grips with a grave crisis linked to environmental decline must be met by the labor and imagination of millions of individuals, working in diverse but complementary ways, animated by a single redemptive vision.

This vision is examined more closely in our final chapter. Here, we look at the dimensions of the present and future environmental cleanup shortfall.

Fudging the Numbers

It quickly becomes clear to anyone researching environmental cleanup costs that as appalling as estimates in this field appear to be, they are almost always understated. Not minimally understated. Not moderately understated. But vastly, hugely and, not infrequently, frighteningly understated.

Part of this understatement, of course, is related to the way officials traditionally break bad news to the public. In the Soviet Union, even under *Glasnost*, news of Chernobyl leaked out very slowly. Even today, people living in areas around the disaster have no access to their own medical records or to the results of the radioactive monitoring Soviet authorities are constantly performing.

In this country news gets out a bit more promptly but, at least in the short run, not always much more accurately. A military cost overrun tends to be reported initially in a way that makes it seem more like a minor oversight than a national outrage. Cutbacks in popular social programs are gilded with hints that lesser expenditures will go further because of more efficient management.

Bad news also tends to be dribbled out so that public tolerance has a chance to rise to appropriate levels of acceptance. When the savings and loan crisis first hit the media in 1987, for example, bailout costs were estimated at $5 billion. By the 1988 presidential campaign, total bailout cost projections had risen to $20 billion.

A few weeks after the election the estimate rose to $50 billion. By early 1989, people in Washington were talking in terms of a round $100 billion. A short while later it was revealed that when interest payments over 10 years were added in, the total was likely to exceed $150 billion, and over 30 years the bill to taxpayers might come to $300 billion or more.

A similar progression took place with estimates of costs to render U.S. nuclear weapons-making facilities and the areas around them safe. When the problem was first announced, $10 billion was the probable cost. That figure has now risen to more than $150 billion, though the magnitude of this expense is often disguised by citing "just" the $50 billion or so it will take to clean up the 12 weapons facilities themselves, exclusive of surrounding terrain.

This same attitude of "Estimate as low as you can get away with today, and let some later Congress or administration take the heat tomorrow," naturally is at work when it comes to projecting costs of all kinds of environmental cleanup. Along with this inevitable bureaucratic ploy, a number of special circumstances are also working to make today's environmental cleanup numbers more likely to be downpayments than final costs.

One of these circumstances has to do with the combination of gushing optimism, deliberate obliviousness and simple oversight, which rendered the true dimensions of many environmental dangers unclear until very recently.

Acknowledging the Problem
May Get Worse

It takes time to assimilate new data or data ignored in the past. It takes time to fully appreciate the true costs of many kinds of cleanup.

With many environmental risks, even officials willing to acknowledge present problems and their costs are often less than anxious to admit these problems may get worse and their solutions more expensive. When facing cleanups of a kind never actually done before, the official bent is to assume that the lowest fix-up estimates will apply.

All of these tendencies are on display when looking at present government predictions concerning the pricetag to protect this country from a single category of pollutants—old solid and aqueous hazardous wastes generated by industry. It is instructive to see how the true cost of environmental cleanup in this one area has been systematically distorted.

Waste Inflation
Run Amok

The federal Superfund has $8.5 billion to spend on old hazardous waste site clean up through 1991. Superfund clean ups, however, are only done at abandoned toxic waste sites where polluters cannot be identified or are no longer in a position to foot the bill.

The vast majority of old toxic waste sites in this country are to be rendered environmentally sound by corporate entities, still in business, who were responsible for the contamination. These sites are where the number fudging with this kind of waste becomes evident.

Preliminary estimates of how much it will cost to clean the 1,200-plus extremely dangerous and toxic Superfund sites on the EPAs priority list range up to $120 million, and now average $21 million each. What makes these numbers even more monstrous than they appear to be at first is that they are so tentative. The truth is that, as of today, we lack difinitive real experience with actual site cleanup. Government estimates of total hazardous-waste cleanup expenses over the next decade or two should be based on past costs to do similar work. Instead, they are little more than guesswork.

Of all sites on EPA's Superfund priority list, just 889 (about two-thirds) had been fully studied at the time of this writing. Between 1980 and May, 1989 only 252 had actually been "cleaned."

Only some 56 EPA-listed toxic-waste site cleanups had yet been paid for with private funds, though privately funded cleanups are supposed to dominate in this field, with the government acting only as payer of last resort. The first agreement to clean up such a site using only private money was not even reached until the mid-1980s.

Given the extreme paucity of experience cleaning old sites, present cost estimates in this realm have little or no substance. What can be said with virtual certainty, however, is that expenditures here will be higher, not lower, when studies give way to actual cleanup work.

Has a government defense program or antipoverty program *ever* come in under budget? Why should anyone expect toxic-site cleanup projects to fare any better in this regard?

Increase of Sites

Another factor that will push up costs: The number of toxic-waste sites that require expensive testing, monitoring and remediation is constantly increasing. The EPA added 101 sites in 33 states to its emergency priority list on April 1, 1989. This brought the total on this list to 1,163.

Such Superfund sites are by no means an inclusive registry of places needing extensive, and frequently costly, remediation work. The EPA also has a list of 28,000 other toxic sites around the country that are not quite bad enough to qualify for emergency attention. Individual states have several times that number on their own toxic-site cleanup lists. Some estimates of the total number of toxic sites in this country that may ultimately require costly cleanup run in excess of 400,000.

In the category of sites not yet listed as *very* toxic but likely to be so listed in years to come, are some facilities currently functioning as landfills. There are about 15,000 operating landfills around this country. A recent government ruling that requires more secure linings to prevent further groundwater contamination around these dumping grounds hints at their state of grace vis-à-vis the surrounding environment—and the probable inclusion of many of them on Superfund lists in years to come.

Another joker in industry's toxic-waste cleanup deck is the vast number of sites not quite bad enough to achieve state or federal toxic-waste status but still requiring some type of cleanup. Many are around leaking underground tanks. You find these contaminated areas near old service stations and abandoned manufacturing facilities from coast to coast.

There are between 500,000 and 700,000 of them. It typically costs between $10,000 and $100,000 to render one environmentally safe.

The U.S. Office of Technology Assessment has estimated it will cost on the order of $500 billion to render benign all the industry-generated toxic waste already in our environment. That estimate is based on present levels of environmental deterioration—on *known* levels. It also does not include inflation "escalators."

When you put together the facts and stats noted above, this is the way it adds up:

- American society is facing a $100-500 billion bill to clean existing seriously toxic waste sites.
- This bill will grow as new sites are created and discovered.
- The number of very dangerous toxic sites around the country is increasing considerably faster than old ones are being cleaned.
- The number of less toxic, but still dangerous, hazardous-waste sites is growing far, far faster than old ones are being cleaned.

The government's Superfund allocations to address this problem—$8.5 billion to be spent between 1987 and 1991—is pathetically inadequate compared with the size of the problem, while private sources, responsible for the bulk of cleanup costs, have yet to make any meaningful contributions.

This is the state of affairs for just one type of environmental risk—old industry-generated solid and liquid toxic wastes. Problems and costs associated with nuclear wastes, utility-generated acid rain, air pollution associated with automobiles and power plants, nontoxic municipal trash disposal, agricultural pesticide contamination and scores of other types of expenditures related to environmental deterioration are equally disturbing.

The primary question that comes to mind here is this: Where is capital of the magnitude necessary to address all these huge and complex problems to come from?

Potato Passing

An old blues lyric goes, "Everybody wants to go to heaven, but nobody wants to die." It is a perfect way to describe our present national attitude toward paying for environment cleanup.

There is no bigger apple-pie issue today than environmentalism. After a decade during which protecting natural systems took a back seat to hang-the-air, hang-the-water development, environmental priorities are again at the forefront of national consciousness.

Established environmental lobbying groups are regaining their vigor and visibility. The pollute-we-must crowd is in full retreat. The general public is up in arms against pollution in all its guises.

The media is covering the environmental scene with the exuberance of repentant sinners. Congress is preparing to crank out new legislation. The administration in Washington is headed by an avowed lover of nature.

Unlike an earlier environmental explosion in the 1970s, this one need not start from ground zero in its approach to problem solving. There is an enormous body of enabling rules and regulations in place to effect changes, and a huge cadre of trained technicians and officials to see that decisions are implemented expeditiously.

A revolutionary spurt of environmental preservation and restoration should now be underway. Instead, the powers-that-be are playing a game of hot potato, diligently focusing on attributing blame for all forms of past and present pollution, so as not to be left holding the 'tater when it comes time to pay this cleanup revolution's massive costs.

The federal government was the great environmental sugar daddy in years past. But it is no longer fiscally able to fill that role. Decades of excessive spending on social programs and even more excessive military outlays have, for all practical purposes, undermined the ability of the national government in Washington to be the generative force behind *any* new crusade, no matter how necessary, no matter how great its constituency.

Even after cost-of-living adjustments are adjusted downward, even after Army, Navy and Air Force requests are pared, just the expense of servicing old debt will render the federal budget inoperative as an instrument of revolutionary change or renewal. The environment will be competing for scarce federal dollars with such health crises as the AIDS epidemic. It will be in the same fund-seeking queue as programs fighting drug use in urban America.

Along with its on-budget obligations, the federal government is burdened with an even larger and potentially more costly series of off-budget commitments. The recent S&L bailout is but one example of these fiscal black holes, any one of which is liable to suck up enormous government treasure if circumstances are right.

Quasi-government agencies backing student loans, farm loans, various forms of real estate loans and a dozen other categories of loans might one day soon be forced to tap federal coffers for salvation. A number of these agencies were in trouble during the relatively fat years of the mid-1980s. Why should anyone suppose they will need less in the way of relief in the early 1990s?

Philosophically, none of these fiscal difficulties and restraints should affect federal environmental spending because, in a philosophical sense, the environment is not a political issue. Politics are an environmental issue. The preeminent needs of natural systems on which all life depends should take precedence over the parochial needs and demands of various national constituencies.

Politicians, however, are not philosophers—at least, not until forced to be. The ones in Washington today will thus sigh heavily at each new manifestation of environmental decline, rhetorically position themselves on the issue so as to look good to the folks back home and, when it comes time to allocate funds for different budgetary priorities, vote in ways that seem best to enhance prospects for reelection.

Even were U.S. voters to demand much more in the way of environmental spending, another, even more powerful group stands ready to veto the move—foreign bankers. The United States no longer has absolute control over its own economic destiny because past overspending has put much of the fiscal sovereignty we once enjoyed into foreign hands.

Our military strength, the special status of our currency and our position as the world's largest consumer of goods and services mean we will never be treated quite the same as Latin American or African debtors by international lending consortia. With respect to Washington's ability to fund a domestic environmental renaissance, however, a belief that foreign bankers will let us off the hook so we can pay to clean up our air and water is naive.

Thus, except for a few well-publicized new programs and modest spending for existing ones, environmental solutions from Washington will not be forthcoming. The only really serious initiatives to be expected from this quarter in years to come will be attempts to pass the environmental cost burden to private industry through stiffer regulations and to the backs of individuals through higher user fees.

Hot Potato

An important tenet of Ronald Reagan's "new federalism" was to give states more responsibilities in all sorts of governmental realms. One of these was the environment. In a certain sense, this transfer of responsibilities has been a success.

There were more than 2,000 bills relating to environmental cleanup introduced in state legislatures in 1988. There are more than 50 percent more staffers working on environmental problems at the level of state government than are employed by the EPA in Washington. The catalog of innovative state programs cited in an earlier chapter of this book hints at the environmental initiatives now coming from state capitals.

State governments, however, are also very active when it comes to trying to shift larger shares of their own environmental burdens to other jurisdictions. To date, almost half the states in the Union have passed laws banning disposal of toxic wastes within their own boundaries, and most others are considering similar measures. One expert in this field has dubbed this process a "civil war."

When it comes to actually allocating more money for environmental cleanup, states are in much the same position today as the federal government. One recent headline summed up this situation perfectly: "States Increase Taxes and Curtail Services as Revenues Dwindle."

In 1984, coming out of a steep recession, state and local governments in this country chalked up a collective surplus of more than $20 billion. In 1988, by way of comparison, the collective deficit of these governments was more than $14 billion.

A few states, especially in the Northeast, are valiantly trying to hold the line when it comes to environmental expenditures. As noted earlier, New Jersey, the country's most polluted state by several measures, continues to increase cleanup funding in its new budget.

The bloom is obviously off the rose for New Jersey's economy in this particular economic cycle, however. In 1989 the Garden State was facing its tightest budgetary squeeze since the recession year of 1982. Obviously, regardless of the hopes and desires of its legislature and governor, its spending on clean air and water will flatten in years to come. Similar situations exist in other environmentally progressive states like Massachusetts and New York, both currently experiencing their own economic decelerations.

Many of the environmental funding problems of state, county and city governments are related to the so-called tax reform movement that has swept the nation since Congress passed its own famous version in 1986. The transformation of federal and local tax codes since then has had a devastating effect on the ability of all local governments to borrow money for environmental cleanup.

So much nonsense has been written about "leveling playing fields," "taking tax shelters away from the rich" and "simplifying the way Americans pay their taxes" that the real import of contemporary tax reform has been largely overlooked. What tax reform is *really* all about is eliminating or reducing the indirect subsidies government has long extended to sectors of the economy deemed socially desirable.

When the world was young and the United States was solvent, federal and state governments could use their tax codes to indirectly subsidize low-income housing, energy exploration, capital equipment investment, research and development, and such projects as new water treatment plants and sewerage systems. These subsidies were administered through "preferences" written into the codes. They were packaged for sale to the wealthy elements of the general public as "tax shelters."

This subsidy system was extraordinarily effective in realizing its goals. When it was in high gear, there were relatively few Americans forced to live in the streets because enough low-cost housing was unavailable. Oil and gas drilling boomed. Vast amounts of money went into research and development. Local governments had no trouble selling environment-related bond issues.

The fact that the federal treasury was also losing billions of dollars to people who abused the preference system by taking excess or spurious deductions in the guise of investing in legitimate shelters was largely irrelevant. The world, after all, was young, and the United States solvent. Why quibble over trifles?

The wholesale destruction of this subsidy system through "tax reform" was every bit as symptomatic of this country's fiscal decline as removal of transportation subsidies in Haiti or meat subsidies in Poland are symptoms of these nations' fiscal despair. The specific effects of tax reform on state and local governments' environmental cleanup efforts is this: Lower marginal tax rates mean federally tax-exempt municipal bonds are less attractive investments. To make them more attractive—i.e., to compensate for reduced federal tax subsidies—issuers of these bonds must raise yields of these securities.

Thus, the cost of state and local environmental borrowing increases. And, because states now face an overall fiscal crunch, they are borrowing less to repair the environment at the same time that they have less tax revenues to spend on this same purpose. At the same time federal revenue sharing related to the environment is also decreasing.

Not surprisingly, the situation at the level of municipal government is even more precarious when it comes to environmental spending. From New York to Seattle, from Madison to Miami, city administrations are inaugurating hundreds of innovative programs and projects aimed at improving local environments. However, only the ones funded directly and indirectly by user fees on business and individuals have much substance, because virtually no large American city now has the economic wherewithal to pay for its own environmental initiatives.

More solid waste will be picked up in New York because of fines levied on shopkeepers who do not sweep in front of their businesses. More trash will be collected in Seattle because of pay-per-barrel pickup practices. More things will be recycled in Philadelphia because of mandated solid-waste segregation. These initiatives, however, are *administered*, not paid for, by cities. They are pass-alongs of environmental costs to somebody else.

Another Hot Potato

In the well-evolved mythology of environmental good guys and bad guys, no group seems as perfectly designed to play the role of the Great Satan as "industry." Industry is the great producer of wastes. Industry is the great dumper of toxics. And, in fact, enough honest-to-goodness examples exist of industry executives deliberately and maliciously fouling the natural environment in ways so despicable they make one ashamed to share a common gene pool that industry and business generally make prime scapegoats for politicians seeking to shift the burden of environmental cleanup.

Certainly, that is what federal, state and local government officials now seek to do in every way possible. That industry as an institutional polluter has simply embodied and expressed the general callous national obsession with making and consuming goods at the expense of environmental preservation is naturally ignored in this effort.

The problem here for would-be burden-shifters is twofold. First, industry is not altogether helpless when it comes to defending itself from officials who would make the private sector pay the environmental due-bill. Second, even when the hot potato is successfully passed along, many businesses simply do not have the money to meet their assigned obligations.

The first line of defense often employed by corporations seeking to escape environmental responsibility is manned by the public-relations department. A corporation's love of nature is detailed in its annual report and through sponsorship of nature shows. Full-page ads pleading economic hardship or "unfairness" are run whenever expensive new environmental compliance seems in the offing.

After the potential of public relations is exhausted, industry turns to lobbying. The aim of this activity is to escape environmental compliance costs completely, spread them over a wider area or shift the burden to the public purse.

The increasingly popular last resort of industrial polluters is to seek protection from environmental obligations through bankruptcy. In a market culture where bankruptcy is frequently used as a tool to boost profits by stiffing retired workers out of health benefits, or to break unobliging unions, it should surprise no one that it is also becoming a popular method of weaseling out of costly environmental commitments.

The corporate thinking that leads to such behavior is really not all that different from the thinking of government officials. People who run governments in this country are afraid to offend constituents by making them pay the costs of their past polluting practices. People who run companies take the same protective stance toward their shareholders.

The notion that obligations to the natural environment might transcend those to constituents or shareholders is one that has yet to permeate our national institutional consciousness. In today's astonishing unevolved business ethical milieu, in fact, companies doing all they can to escape paying their environmental fair share fit in perfectly.

And Another Hot Potato

In what might be called an intracorporate battle over who owes what in this realm, the insurance industry is going head-to-head with some of its largest business customers. The battle is taking places in scores of courtrooms. It is also taking place on newspaper business pages, where one of the country's biggest commercial and industrial insurance underwriters began running ads in early 1989 calling for the establishment of a National Environmental Trust

Fund. Not surprisingly, such a fund, among other things, would moderate the environmental burdens of insurers.

Hot Potato, Again!

Even were the different elements of corporate America suddenly smitten with a desire to cleanse the air and waters, there are serious questions about their ability to do so. After a decade of mergers and acquisitions, many funded with high interest junk bonds, the debt load of American business is 30 percent above historical norms.

Many firms now find it difficult to keep facilities open and have a little left over for R&D after servicing their debt. Where is the leftover "fat" for environmental cleanup to come from?

An inability to confront the implications of this question largely explains why, except for those environmental challenges that cannot be ignored, most corporations today simply hide their heads in the sand on this issue and hope like hell that it will go away. As astounding as it may seem, given the pervasive nature of environmental deterioration, almost no major American corporations have yet taken environmental changes on their balance sheets (i.e., formally set aside funds for future environmental cleanup costs) for which the companies will certainly be liable at some future date nonetheless.

Thousands and thousands of other companies in this country with serious environmental liabilities are afraid to take this step. Since auditors, rating services and the Securities and Exchange Commission do not yet require such a step to be taken, in the same way that set-asides are required to fund future pension obligations, such an attitude makes tenuous, temporary sense—though from a long-term fiscal perspective, it is absolutely insane.

How great is corporate America's total environmental liability? A front-page *Wall Street Journal* article in May 1988 put the figure at $100 billion—though an EPA official quoted in the piece acknowledged this was likely on the low side. As noted above, some other government agencies have estimated that just the solid and liquid hazardous wastes produced by industry in years past may cost five times that much to render harmless.

Even $100 billion, however, is more than the combined 1987 profits of all companies in the Fortune 500. Even taking this low-ball total as the most accurate estimate of the cost to clean up the wastes specifically generated by American business—and even if cleanup payments are spaced over considerable periods of time—the money needed to clean up old wastes, at the same time paying the costs of limiting newly generated varieties, is simply beyond the capacity of the American business community.

This is the heart of the great environmental hot potato game now being played out in newspapers and on the floors of legislatures around the country. It is at the heart of endless courtroom battles, in which manufacturers sue insurers for damages to cover their own environmental liabilities, in which states sue the federal government to perform (and pay for) some environmental task, in which activist lawyers sue governments or companies to make them do things statutes say they ought to do.

Having spent the better part of the last two decades monitoring and defining environmental problems, the time has finally arrived to pay for their solutions. And nobody has the bread.

Taking Sides

Thousands of toxic sites riddle this land like malignancies, many of which might spread with fearful consequences if not treated promptly. But the patient does not have the wherewithal to pay for necessary treatments, and the attending physicians, whose past efforts are largely responsible for the present crisis, stand around the bedside arguing and pointing fingers.

In the failures of government and business to honestly confront our present environmental difficulties, one sees the harbingers of fearsome change. Ultimately, even the strongest political and economic institutions—historically grounded, able to tap deep wells of traditional support—will fall away and be replaced if they cannot provide water that is drinkable, air one can breathe and safe places in which to live and work.

The destabilizing effects of environmental decline are not as obvious yet in the United States as they are in the Soviet Union, where resurgent regional nationalisms are more and more fueled by a recognition of damages wrought by Moscow's central planners on regional ecologies. But a similar, if still less clearcut, trend is developing on these shores.

The present paralysis of established institutions when it comes to coping with pollution of all kinds is spawning a revolutionary fury. Some 12,000 organizations now make up the responsible, respectable environmental community in this country. But in their shadow a still disorganized and nebulous environmental *doppelgänger* is coming into being. Its members have seen their children born with fearful defects associated with chemical contamination, the national landscape they love turning rank and gray, their economic opportunities packaged as an enemy of nature.

The anger of these people, the righteous force they represent, will one day find an institutional channel. Whether that channel is compatible with the kind of society we currently enjoy remains to be seen.

At present, understanding and employing the environmental factor is one of the very few ways people can effectively confront and combat environmental decline. What institutions are unwilling or unable to do, individuals, as consumers and investors, as executives and entrepreneurs, are moving to achieve.

A self-indulgent babbittry was the economic ideal of the decade now ending. Individual economic efforts had no purpose beyond facilitating the purchase of progressively more expensive products and services. Now, the environmental factor once more links individual economic success with higher ends.

In a political context, the environmental factor is an important mechanism in preserving the integrity of our society until the current crop of impotent and confused leadership is replaced by a more environmentally sound assemblage that has its priorities in proper perspective.

The transformations in individual thinking wrought by the environmental factor, which will help bring about these necessary economic and political transformations, are discussed in the next chapter.

CHAPTER 14

Environmental Alchemy and Personal Transformation

When most people think of alchemy, they think of the quest to turn base metals into gold. Alchemists are visualized as badly informed medieval chemists mixing secret ingredients in pursuit of impossible dreams, usually in the service of hard-up royalty looking for an easy solution to financial difficulties.

There is more than a little truth in these notions. But there is also more to traditional alchemy than bad science and simple greed.

Many alchemists were practicing a spiritual exercise at the same time they were seeking physical and chemical transformations. The rites of purification they performed on "base" metals to change them into "higher" metals were outward expressions of purifications they were seeking to work on themselves.

Each step in the metal-changing process was accompanied by prayer, fasting and meditation. Each sign that something was happening in beakers and mortars was a sign that something was happening in the alchemist's own spiritual development.

Alchemy Put to Use

In looking at the consequences of employing the environmental factor, a similar progression becomes evident. Yes, it helps preserve natural systems. Yes, it improves one's personal solvency and work effectiveness. But it transforms the psyche of the user as well.

There is no more pernicious—and silly—dictum of Marxism than the one that holds that people are primarily motivated by economic forces. In spite of the "nonmaterial" incentives that have led literally billions of people in our own century to make choices that have worked directly against their personal economic interests—choices ranging from willful acceptance of totalitarian and fundamentalist life-styles to sacrifices made to keep these life-styles from sweeping over everyone else—much of the thinking world still feels obliged to pretend that a desire for more money is the only thing that makes people tick.

Once this dubious premise is accepted, a stock tip that makes one money is deemed all right, even if the boost in a stock's price is at the expense of workers' jobs. A management technique that saves a few dollars in environmental costs is deemed fine if it gives one an edge in the corporate hierarchical struggle, even if it also leads to a bit more corporate pollution being loosed on the environment.

The fact that these approaches may take a psychic toll on the "winners" in these transactions is beyond the scope of much modern personal financial thinking. The fact that even in the narrowest economic sense many of these approaches do not make a whit of sense is conveniently overlooked as well.

Ethics aside, the relationship between removing government subsidies for low-cost housing and the extra personal costs to working people that result from this policy because their parents move in or their grown children cannot afford to move out is fairly obvious. So, too, are the higher property taxes to haul away trash and the cost of lost work days from bronchitis that result when environmental concerns are sloughed off.

Virtually all the pass-alongs to a later generation that a society can possibly get away with have been passed along by our own generation. Especially with respect to the environment, we no longer have the option to burden our children and our children's children with our sins. Today, the victims of additional pollution are ourselves.

A philosophy of personal finance that does not take into account the immediate, personal consequences individual decisions now have on macroeconomic systems, which in turn "trickle back" to affect millions and millions of individual economic existences, is at least a decade out of sync with the times.

It has always been true that what goes around comes around. Now, with so many economic and ecological systems saturated with the effluent of our past excesses, the time lag between going around and coming around when it comes to both the economy and the environment is virtually zero.

That is why the environmental factor is not only a more "fulfilling," socially responsible personal economic philosophy but a more psychically enriching one as well. It is also why the personal transformation it helps bring about transcends the economic realm altogether and brings people closer to the core of themselves.

Among ecologists and biologists, deepening knowledge of the interrelatedness of natural forces and populations can lead to visions of wholeness. The same can be said of practitioners of other scientific disciplines. For the rest of us—less intuitive, less specialized in our vocations—the road to this understanding must come from everyday activities infused with the potential to exalt. If we are to be transformed in ways that make the hours of our days precious, the basic components of these days—working, spending, planning better ways to get more from both—must be the mechanisms of our transformation.

This is the alchemy of the environmental factor. This is the meld of economic life to Life. This is the resolution of the schism between personal economic assertion and higher responsibility—a resolution that has finally come about because no other resolution is any longer possible.

In the last chapter, we noted the current monetary and moral impoverishment of American (and many international) institutions that renders them incapable of meeting the greatest challenge of our century—the salvation of the physical environment. At some time, of course, these same institutions will have to participate in achieving this end. They now lag behind mass individual transformation in this realm because fundamental institutional perceptional evolution always trails individual evolution on important matters.

Today's captains of industry rose to their present positions by abusing the environment, not by protecting it. The idea that top corporate executives who have spent the past thirty years ignoring environmental strictures or manipulating them to their own advantage would suddenly announce at this year's annual meeting the establishment of a huge reserve to cover past and future company liabilities at the expense of next decade's corporate profitability is ludicrous.

Political leaders did not rise to their present posts by environmental zeal, either. Environmentalism has been "an issue" for more than 20 years, but it has not been a gut issue like employment or inflation. It has not been an issue to stake a candidacy on. It has been merely an issue to fill out an agenda and win a few extra votes that might be leaning.

With respect to the environment, the basic flaw of our present crop of leaders, both economic and political, is that they still suffer from what might be called the "King Canute syndrome." Canute was an 11th-century monarch who at various times ruled over England and large patches of Scandinavia. He was a famous warrior, law-giver and protector of church property. His major flaw was vanity. And it was a demonstration of this flaw that has kept his name alive to our own time. We remember him today because of his vain attempt to assert his hege-mony over the natural elements in his domains, including the ocean around England.

It was a perfectly normal thing to do—from Canute's perspective. He ruled. Everything in his domain was therefore subject to his wishes. Gathering his court, which included priests whose job it was to bring God into line with the king's whims, Canute marched down to the sea and ordered it to stop washing up on his beaches.

This is pretty much the same attitude and approach taken by American business and political leaders vis-à-vis the environment. From their perspective, nature must somehow conform to the requirements of human com-merce and electoral pressures. If environmental spending and enforcement offend more important economic and po-litical interests, nature must make way.

That we must adapt to imperatives of the natural or-der rather than vice-versa is simply outside their ken or beyond their will. That we live in the natural world as a fe-tus lives in the womb of its mother, and that as a fetus that poisons its mother destroys itself, is a concept that still strikes most of them as an outrageous intrusion on their traditional prerogatives.

The best that most business and political leaders in this country (and most everywhere else) can manage when forced, kicking and squealing, to a semblance of recogni-tion of the dangers that environmental deterioration rep-resents to every aspect of human civilization, is a grudging willingness to "cut a deal with nature." If CFCs destroy the ozone layer, they are phased out over 10 years, a period lengthy enough so big producers can reposition themselves without undue discomfort—except, of course, in countries like the Soviet Union, where it would be too inconvenient to take even this step, or in developing nations like India or China, where officials continue to hold out for some kind of "reward" for participating in a plan aimed at saving an environmental barrier necessary for all human life.

If the air is foul and acid rain blights the land, emissions are cut. But they are cut only after years and years of debate, and then, a bit at a time and in ways that do not overly upset mining or utility interests.

If new rules of any kind aimed at protecting the environment are introduced, and if they should happen to threaten the interests of anyone in the United States, the matter generally becomes a subject of litigation. Costly and lengthy litigation that conforms to the highest judicial standards of "due process" is the priority. Prompt intervention to save or remediate natural systems waits upon the convenience of the courts.

This is the King Canute Syndrome. If the waves cannot actually be stopped, surely they can be flattened a bit. Surely, in Canute's kingdom, the forces of nature will subordinate themselves to the more important needs, precepts, institutions and authority of man.

The Way Things Are

One day, our present crop of Canutes will be replaced in leadership positions by individuals whose first entry in society's ledger books will be the Environment. All other debits and credits will be assigned a priority only after this primary obligation is fully and honestly satisfied.

For the time being, this budding leadership is still training—Learning its way, sharpening its skills, cultivating a vision, and being transfigured by that vision.

For the natural environment to be saved and the best elements of our civilization to be retained in the process, however, more than a cadre of heroes and heroines will be needed. Only the day-to-day commitment and intelligence of myriad men and women, performing the millions and millions of little tasks that alone provide any real hope to save a situation of extraordinary dimensions, can do the job. This world will be saved from the bottom up, not from the top down, or it will not be saved at all.

When another low, dishonest decade was drawing to a close, the poet William Auden wrote that "We must love each other or die." He was referring to the need of people to care for their fellows, so that all might be saved from the mass destruction of war.

Today, given the state of the natural environment, it might fairly be said that we must love *everything* or die.

This is not a choice. Nor is it merely a "best alternative." It is not a notion that applies only to those with an aesthetic preference for green grass over downtown skylines.

This is postnaturalist environmentalism. This is survival-mandated environmentalism. This is reality, henceforth and forever after.

A P P E N D I X

There are many specific questions that people employing the environmental factor might wish to ask sellers of real estate, stocks and bonds. Here are some general sample questions to ask when considering purchase of any of these assets.

Residential Real Estate Checklist:

1. Are there any sites on the federal Superfund list in the area?
2. Are there any landfills, trash transfer facilities, private or municipal incineration plants, or nuclear plants in the area?
3. Have local property taxes gone up in the past few years because of rising costs of disposing of locally generated trash?
4. If there are old, abandoned industrial sites in the neighborhood, what kind of wastes were produced at those sites when they were operational?

5. If there are abandoned gas stations in the neighborhood, have their underground tanks been removed?
6. Do a surprising number of people in this area seem to use bottled water?
7. What does the local municipal water district say about general water quality in this area?
8. Does local zoning prevent environmentally "unpleasant" neighbors from moving into the area in years to come?
9. Is there nearby federal, state or privately controlled conservancy land in the area that will *never* generate local pollution?
10. How many days was the area in which this house stands out of compliance with federal air-quality regulations?
11. In terms of possible indoor contamination, has the house been checked for radon?
12. Has the tap water been analyzed?
13. What sort of insulation material is used in this house?
14. Is there asbestos around the piping, the water heater, etc.?

Stock Checklist:

1. Does the industry of which your company is a part have especially great environmental exposure (petrochemical, etc.)?
2. Has it, in fact, been subject to numerous and costly environment-related fines in recent years?
3. Aside from expressions of concern by top management, what specific steps has the company taken to reduce its environmental exposure in recent years?

4. Does it have a reserve set aside for environmental mishaps not covered by insurance?
5. Is a large part of the company's "outside" coverage actually self-insurance?
6. Are many company facilities located in states with strict environmental laws? And if so, has the company run afoul of state environmental officials in years past?
7. If the company has extensive environmental exposure, has it taken steps to offset this exposure by setting up or buying environmental cleanup affiliates?
8. Does the company own old facilities that may cost a lot to environmentally clean in the future?
9. If the firm under consideration is an environmental services company, does it derive most of its income from Fortune 500 firms or government contracts? (The latter are more susceptible to spending cutbacks.)
10. Is this environmental services firm "full-service" and well-established in many sectors of the business, or is it too dependent on a single technology, contract, patent, or service?
11. How much of the insurance risk associated with this environmental services company's operations is actually protected by nonaffiliated insurance carriers?

Bonds Checklist:

1. If an investment-grade corporate issue, does the issuer have very serious environmental exposure that could affect its future ability to service debt?

2. If a junk corporate issue, does the issuer have so much environmental exposure that a marginal offering becomes unacceptably risky?
3. If a foreign bond, does the country issuing the bond have very serious environmental problems that make it more likely to default?
4. If a junk municipal issue, is the facility whose revenues are supposed to service the bond debt the sort whose operations might be negatively affected by pollution problems?

BIBLIOGRAPHY

Most of the material in this book is gleaned from newspaper and magazine articles, annual reports, newsletters, speeches, government and trade group studies and the like. The reason is that such current sources are where the environmental economics story is being told today. A substantial book literature in this field is yet to appear—though this will doubtless change shortly.

Among books about the environment with a generally noneconomic focus, but which nonetheless touch on "The Environmental Factor" in ways readers of this book might find useful, the author especially recommends: Lester R. Brown (Ed.) *State of the World*, Washington, D.C., Worldwatch Institute, 1989. In terms of prophetic work about the future of the world if environmental concerns are not recognized, E.F. Schumacher's *Small is Beautiful; economics as of people mattered* (New York, Harper & Row, 1973) is certainly worth re-reading.

Among the few books in print that touch more directly on "environmental economics" are: Herman E. Daly (Ed.) *Economics, Ecology, Ethics—Essays Toward a Steady State Economy*, San Francisco, W.H. Freeman and Co.,

1980; and Tom Tietenberg, *Environmental and Natural Resource Economics*, Glenview, IL., Scott Foresman and Co., 1984.

Certain monthly publications give one a good feel for the economic scope of environmental deterioration. They include *Greenpeace* magazine and Worldwatch's own periodical, *World Monitor.*

There are hundreds of groups and organizations turning out publications which to a greater or lesser extent examine facets of the environmental-economic relationship. Among the author's own favorite sources in this realm are the Edison Electric Institute, Washington, D.C.; the New Alchemy Institute, East Falmouth, MA., and Sierra Club Books, San Francisco, CA. A great number of other nonprofit organizations also produce interesting materials touching on this relationship. They include The Environmental Defense Fund and the Environmental Law Institute in New York City and Washington, D.C. respectively.

The Environmental Protection Agency, of course, along with dozens of other governmental bodies, also publishes many works that touch on this realm with varying degrees of directness. To get a list of available EPA publications, readers can contact the National Technical Information Service, 5285 Port Royal Road, Springfield, VA. 22161.

The Council of State Governments turns out a *Resource Guide to State Environmental Management* which the author found useful in understanding the scope and responsibilities of local governments' environmental practices. The Council's address is Iron Works Pike, P.O. Box 11910, Lexington, KY 40578-9989.

To this author's way of thinking, an unusual, but exceptionally valuable, source of economic insights related to environmental decline is the annual reports issued by companies in the environmental services industry. Such companies have a vested interest in knowing the economic costs of pollution and describing to their shareholders the extent of economic damage done to ecosystems.

More than 100 such reports were perused in preparing this book. Among those I suggest as good environmental economics data sources are annuals from:

Browning-Ferris Industries, Houston, TX. (NYSE/BFI)
Calgon Carbon Corporation, Robinson Township, PA. (NASDAQ/CRBN)
ENSR Corporation, Houston, TX. (ASE/ENX)
Groundwater Technology, Norwood, MA. (NASDAQ/GWTI)
Gundle Environmental Systems, Houston, TX (ASE/GUN)
Jacobs Engineering Group, Pasadena, CA. (ASE/JEC)
Metcalf & Eddy Companies, Branchburg, New Jersey (NASDAQ/METC)
Pacific Nuclear Systems, Federal Way, WA. (NASDAQ/PACN)
Rollins Environmental Systems, Wilmington, DE. (NYSE/REN)
Safety-Kleen Corporation, Elgin, IL (NYSE/SK)
Tech/Ops Landauer, Glenwood, IL. (ASE/TO)
Versar, Inc., Springfield,, VA. (ASE/VSR)
Roy F. Weston, Inc., West Chester, PA. (NASDAQ/WSTNA)
Waste Management, Inc., Oak Brook, IL. (NYSE/WMX)
Wheelabrator Technologies, Danvers, MA. (NASDAQ/WHTI)
Zurn Industries, Erie, PA. (NYSE/ZRN)

Good descriptions of the environmental services industry and the problems it addresses are to be found in analysts' evaluations now being prepared for brokerage houses around the country. Many brokerage firms have their own favorites in this field now. A number offer special reports addressed to the general public, for example, Merrill Lynch's "Cleaning Up Our Polluted Planet: Investment Opportunities in Pollution Control." A more comprehensive guide from this perspective is to be found in the author's own *Directory of Environmental Investing* (Silver Spring, Md: Business Publications, Inc., 1989).

Yet another superb source of up-to-date information about environmental problems and their economic consequences is trade journals. Regular reading of *Chemical Week, ENR, Chemical and Engineering News, Modern Plastics, Constructor, Science* and almost any good real estate monthly is most instructive in this area.

There are also some informative newsletters that regularly touch on various aspects of the environment-economy relationship. The three big publishers in this field today are Business Publishers, Inc., Silver Spring, Maryland (*Air/Water Pollution Report, Hazardous Waste News, Solid Waste Report* and *Environmental Economics*); Inside Washington Publishers, Washington, D.C. (*Insider EPA*); and Bureau of National Affairs, Washington, D.C. (*Environmental Reporter*).

The waste industry has its own trade organizations, which produce a slew of reports, studies, etc. The best data here are probably to be obtained from the Air and Waste Management Association, Pittsburgh, Pennsylvania; the Water Pollution Control Foundation, Washington, D.C.; and the National Solid Wastes Management Association, Washington, D.C.

Other trade groups are currently running hundreds of seminars on specialized areas in which environmental change is affecting their own memberships. A fairly typical example is the programs on hazardous waste management and legal liability offered by the Committee on Continuing Professional Education, American Law

Institute–American Bar Association. Related specialized literature from such organizations is generally available.

Leading companies in industries other than waste management often generate valuable information (and views) about the costs of pollution. A speech before the National Press Club in March 1989 by Maurice R. Greenberg, president, American International Group (an insurance company), illustrates this point. Facts cited in that presentation are distributed in several chapters of this book.

Increasingly, international organizations are producing their own data about spreading pollution and its dollar toll. Some very interesting insights are found in reports and papers from the World Bank, the World Commission on Environment and Development, the United Nations Environment Programme and the World Resources Institute.

The best elements of the business press are, of course, superb suppliers of timely data about environmental economics. The author's own favorites are those old reliables, *The Wall Street Journal, New York Times, Forbes* and *The Economist.*

Beyond the books, reports, and government and trade studies used in writing this book, more than a thousand daily newspaper and magazine articles from scores of publications contributed facts cited in these pages. Most of this coverage was of the standard (and often ephemeral) "Today, the EPA announced..." genre. The nearly 100 pieces listed below, however, are more substantial in terms of the way they cover the environmental-economy relationship.

These articles may have more than passing value for anyone seeking to understand how a fast-changing environment is shaping the U.S. and world economies. For easier reference, these citations are divided according to their contributions to different book chapters.

Chapter 1

"U.S. Complaints on Amazon Destruction Spur Brazil's Resentment and Defiance." *The Wall Street Journal*, 2/17/89.

"Is Poland Lost?" *Greenpeace*, 10/11/88.

"Industrialized Eastern Bloc Faces Pollution Crisis." *New York Times*, 10/25/88.

"Pollution Casts Pallor of Death Across the North Sea." *Philadelphia Inquirer*, 9/13/88.

"Europe's Failing Effort to Exile Toxic Trash." *The New York Times*, 10/16/88.

"Suddenly, the World Itself Is a World Issue." *The New York Times*, 12/25/88.

"Ecologists Make Friends with Economists." *The Economist*, 10/15/88.

"Deforesting the Earth." *World Watch*, 1/2/89.

"Living in Chernobyl's Shadow, They Demand the Truth." *Philadelphia Inquirer*, 2/26/89.

"Brazil Wants Its Dams, but at What Costs." *The New York Times*, 3/12/89.

"A Day of Reckoning Nears as Vast Plains Aquifer Ebbs." *Boston Globe*, 8/29/85.

"African Nations Barring Toxic Waste." *The New York Times*, 9/25/88.

"Laden with Every Sort of Refuse, the Ocean Has Become a Trash Bin." *The New York Times*, 11/22/87.

"Troubled Waters." *Business Week*, 10/12/87.

"Ecologists See Warnings in Sea Pollution Incidents." *The New York Times*, 9/13/87.

"The Hole at the Bottom of the World." *The New York Times*, 9/19/87.

"CFC Curb to Save Ozone Will Be Costly." *The Wall Street Journal*, 3/28/88.

"Planet of the Year/Endangered Earth." *Time* magazine, 1/2/89.

Chapter 2

"New Jersey at Forefront on Landfill Legislation." *Trenton Times,* 8/29/88.

"The Economics of the Waste Crisis." *The New York Times,* 10/23/88.

"The Trash Mess Won't Be Easily Disposed Of." *The Wall Street Journal,* 12/15/88.

"How To Clean Up Superfund's Act." *The Wall Street Journal,* 9/15/88.

"The Growing Debate over Waste Ash." *Philadelphia Inquirer,* 3/6/89.

"Incineration—A Burning Issue." *Chemical Business,* 10/88.

"The New Wave of Incinerators." *The New York Times,* 2/12/89.

"Deadline Here, but Urban Air Still Foul." *Philadelphia Inquirer,* 8/30/88.

"Clearing the Cloudy State Cleanup Act." *The New York Times,* 2/19/89.

"Reagan and Environment: to Many, a Stalemate." *The New York Times,* 1/1/89.

"Delaware Bay: Environmental Success Story." *Delaware State News,* 2/12/89.

"The Environment as Local Jurisdiction." *The New York Times,* 1/22/89.

Managing Hazardous Waste Risks Under the Massachusetts 'Superfund' Law." *Environmental Progress,* 11/87.

Legislative Avalanche: 2,000 Solid Waste Bills." *BioCycle,* 2/89.

Government Cracks Down on Environmental Crime." *The Wall Street Journal*, 2/16/89.

Chapter 3

"The Worst Beach Pollution Is Routine." *The New York Times*, 9/18/88.

"Novel Efforts to Settle Asbestos Claims Fail as Law Suits Multiply." *The Wall Street Journal*, 6/7/88.

"The Nuclear Arms Industry's Ills, Step by Step." *The New York Times*, 1/8/89.

"Critics Assail Energy Agency on Toxic Waste." *The Wall Street Journal*, 10/19/88.

"Pollution Took Toll on Tourism at Shore, Study Shows." *Philadelphia Inquirer*, 11/5/88.

"Crop and Tree Damage Are Tied to Air Pollution." *The New York Times*, 9/11/88.

"White Wash: The Dioxin." *Greenpeace*, 3/89.

"Declining Water Quality Threatening Coastal Fisheries." *Philadelphia Inquirer*, 11/2/87.

"An Insurance Crisis for Polluters." *Philadelphia Inquirer*, 1/12/88.

"Hot Spots." *New York Times*, 10/23/88.

"Suddenly, Nuclear Waste Looks Very Visible Again." *The New York Times*, 9/18/88.

"Ten Years Later TMI's Neighbors Await Answers." *Philadelphia Inquirer*, 3/28/89.

"A New Kind of Mining Disaster." *The New York Times*, 2/5/89.

"Toxic Chemicals, the Right Response." *The New York Times*, 11/13/88.

"Chemical Firms Press Campaign to Dispel Their 'Bad Guy' Image." *The Wall Street Journal*, 9/20/88.

"The Toxic Morass in Denver's Backyard." *Business Week*, 1/9/89.

"Ozone Defender." *In Business*, 6/88.

"Pollution Fight Takes Aim at Gasoline." *Philadelphia Inquirer*, 3/19/89.

"Big Courtroom for Toxic Web." *The New York Times*, 10/16/87.

"Coming of Age of the Environmental Lawyer." *The New York Times*, 4/29/88.

Chapter 4

"Health Risk from Smog Is Growing, Official Says." *The New York Times*, 2/28/89.

"A Pregnancy Study." *American Journal of Public Medicine*, 6/88.

"EPA Reassesses the Link Between Cancer, Chemicals." *Philadelphia Inquirer*, 2/23/89.

"How the Lung Reacts to Ozone Pollution." *The New York Times*, 8/21/88.

Chapter 5

"Even After 10 Years, Victims of Love Canal Can't Quite Escape It." *The Wall Street Journal*, 10/22/88.

"Conservationists Turn to Tough Tactics." *The New York Times*, 2/26/89.

"Radon Becomes a Real Estate Problem." *Philadelphia Inquirer*, 2/19/88.

"Real Estate Market: Low Tide at Shore." *Philadelphia Inquirer*, 5/29/88.

"Buyers Beware: Not All Real Estate Is Still Good Investment." *Sylvia Porter's Personal Finance Magazine*, 5/87.

"Real Life Horror Story." *Forbes,* 12/12/88.

"Protecting Health in Realty Transactions." *The New York Times,* 2/21/88.

"Indoor Air Quality in Public Buildings." U.S. Environmental Protection Agency, EPA/600/56-88/009a&b.

Chapter 6

"Advances Propel Solar Energy into Market." *The New York Times,* 11/13/88.

"As Northeast's Need for Energy Grows, Gas Becomes a Natural." *The Wall Street Journal,* 2/16/89.

Chapter 7

"How Municipal Bonds Went from Cash Cow to a White Elephant." *The Wall Street Journal,* 12/4/87.

Muny-bond Industry Glumly Tightens Belt." *Philadelphia Inquirer,* 11/7/87.

"Treacherous Times in the Bond Market." *The New York Times,* 3/5/89.

"Beware of Municipal Junk Bonds." *The New York Times,* 12/11/88.

Chapter 8

"Fighting the Greenhouse Effect." *The New York Times,* 8/28/88.

"What Man Has Done to a Hospitable Planet." *The New York Times,* 10/22/88.

"Swept Away." *World Watch,* 1/2/89.

"Mending the Earth's Shield" *World Watch,* 1/2/89.

Chapter 9

"Coping with the Environmental Factor." *Suburban West*, 2/89.

"The Environment and Company Real Estate." *Suburban West*, 4/89.

Chapter 10

"Environmental Employment." *Suburban West*, 6/29.

Environmental Opportunities (all issues). Environmental Studies Department, Antioch/New England Graduate School, Keene, N.H.

"Aluminum Becomes Prime Target of Thieves." *The New York Times*, 2/19/89.

Chapter 11

"Profiting from a Bitter Harvest." *Philadelphia Inquirer*, 3/17/89.

"Two Million Tanks." *In Business*, 1/2/89.

"Big Firms Get High on Organic Gardening." *The Wall Street Journal*, 3/21/89.

"Seeds of Renewal." *World Monitor*, 6/89.

Metrogro Sludge Program Boosts Farm Profits." *Bio-Cycle*, 2/89.

"Radon Warning Is Music to Ears of Testing Firms." *Philadelphia Inquirer*, 9/18/88.

"Is There a Foe in Your Faucet?" *The New York Times*, 7/30/87.

"Jumping in with the Giants." *In Business*, 11/12/88.

"Blue Buckets May Be in New Yorkers' Future." *The New York Times*, 3/16/89.

"What's New in Diapers?" *The New York Times,* 3/12/89.

"Advances in Collecting Plastics." *BioCycle,* 2/89.

"Recycled Rubber Roads." *BioCycle,* 2/89.

"What's New in Recycled Plastics." *The New York Times,* 9/25/88.

Chapter 12

The newspaper sources used in this chapter are cited in the chapter itself.

Chapter 13

"Can $100 Billion Have 'No Material Effect' on Balance Sheets?" *The Wall Street Journal,* 3/11/88.

"The Early Returns of a Toxic Poll." *The New York Times,* 10/20/88.

"Yes to Clean Air, but at What Cost?" *The New York Times,* 3/26/89.

"States Increase Taxes and Curtail Services as Revenues Dwindle." *The Wall Street Journal,* 2/21/89.

INDEX

A

Acadia National Park, 50
Acid rain, 48, 49, 54
Adirondack Mountains, 49
Adriatic Sea, 7
Aflatoxin, 46
Africa, 7,8
Agribusiness, 47
Agriculture (and the
  environment), 45-49, 120
AIDS, 44, 67, 187
Air pollution costs, 12, 51,
  65-66
Aldicarb, 46
Amazonia, 9
Antarctic, 10
Aral Sea, 5
Asbestos, 20, 56, 79, 93, 106,
  130, 147, 153
Ashland Oil, 42, 56
Asia, 8
AT&T, 44, 135-136
Atlantic Richfield Co. (ARCO),
  44
Automobile emissions, 50-52

B

Bangladesh, 8, 121
Banks (and the environmental
  factor), 57-58, 152
Betz Laboratories, 88
Bhopal, 42, 56, 133
Bilbao (Spain), 7
Black Sea, 7
Bonds (and the environmental
  factor), 19, 53, 109-118
Borneo, 8

Boston Harbor, 33, 49, 167
Bottled water, 99
Bowdoin College, 151
Brazil, 9, 113
Browning- Ferris, Inc., 70, 88
Bush administration, 13, 54

C

Calgon Carbon Corp., 88
California, 28, 32, 116, 134
Canada, 10, 54
Cancer, 66, 68, 73, 98
Canonie Environmental
  Services, Inc., 44, 88
Carson, Rachel, 26
Chernobyl, 5, 53, 122
Chesapeake Bay, 49
Chile, 175
China, 8, 121
Chlorofluorocarbons (CFCs),
  44, 66, 115
"Chronic health care crisis,"
  67, 69
Clean Air Act, 26, 29, 30
Clean Harbors, Inc., 88
Clorox Co., 99
Clothing (and the
  environment), 161-162
Coal, 54, 60
Commercial real estate, 57,
  131-133
Commodities (and the
  environmental factor), 119-
  124
Composting, 165
Computers, 58, 102-103
Conservancy movement, 24,
  83

Conservationism, 24
Coors (Adolph) Co., 99
Corporate relocation (and the environment), 138-141
Czechoslovakia, 6

D

Davis Water & Waste, Inc., 88
DDT, 47
Denver, 51
Department of Agriculture, 27
Department of Defense, 27
Department of Energy, 27, 53
"Designer garbage," 167
Dioxins, 59, 73
Drinking water cleanup costs, 12
DuPont, 42, 43, 44, 114

E

East Germany, 6
Economists (and the environment), 4, 173-177
"Ecotopic" communities, 163
Electricity rates, 54
Entrepreneurs (and the environment), 19, 20, 155-169
Environmental employment, 28, 143- 154
Environmental fines, 95-96, 132
Environmental Protection Agency (EPA), 13, 26, 27, 28, 31, 32, 37-38, 41, 46, 58, 66, 68, 76, 79, 81, 93, 120, 127, 129, 132, 133, 144, 183- 184
Environmental regulation, 23-39
Estonia, 6
"Ethical investing", 17-18

Executive planning (and the environmental factor), 127-141
Exxon, 42-43, 56, 114

F

Federal Republic of Germany (West Germany), 6, 16, 92
"Filthadelphia", 25
Fishing (commercial), 49
Florida, 35
Food & Drug Administration, 27

G

General Electric, 44
Gore (Albert, Jr.), 120
Grace (W.R. & Co.), 44
Great Lakes, 49
Greenhouse effect, 45, 120, 121
Green Movement, 16, 48
Greenpeace, 59, 82, 141
Gresham, Sir Thomas, 17

H

Haiti, 8, 191
Health (and the environment), 65-70, 79
Hospitals, 69

I

India, 8, 123, 156-157, 163
Industrial real estate, 78
Insurance (and the environment), 54-57, 94, 105-106

Integrated pest management, 47
Internal Revenue Service, 27, 103
Ireland, 7

J

Japan, 92, 122
Junk Bonds, 113-114, 116-117, 194

K

Kiefer, Anselm, 151
"King Canute syndrome", 203-204
Kodak (Eastman), 114, 115

L

Land and Water Conservation Fund, 83
Lawyers (and environmental litigation), 16, 37, 60-61, 73-74, 195-196
"Liability crisis", 55, 904
Long Island, 50, 75
Love Canal, 20, 72, 73

M

Madagascar, 8
Madison (Wisconsin), 35-36
Malaysia, 8
"Market environmentalism", 17, 141
Massachusetts, 33, 56, 78, 190
Merrill Lynch, 89
Mexico, 9-10, 66
Mining (and the environment), 59

Motor Carrier Act, 30
Monsanto Co., 43
Municipal bonds, 15, 115-116
Municipalities (and the environment), 35-57

N

Naples, 9
National Environmental Trust Fund, 194
Netherlands, /, 16
New Deal, 25
New Jersey, 32-33, 49, 51, /4, 77, 78, 117, 131, 136, 152, 189- 190
New Jersey Institute of Technology, 151
New York City, 36-37, 117
New York State, 34, 37, 117
North Sea, 7
Nuclear power plants, 19
Nuclear waste costs, 12, 27, 52- 54, 181

O

Occidental Petroleum, 42
Occupational Safety & Health Act (OSHA), 30, 31
Oder River, 6
Ohio, 37, 51
OPEC, 20
Organic food, 146, 159-161
Ozone, 11, 50, 66, 115, 140

P

Pakistan, 121
Pennsylvania, 33-34, 37, 116
Perrier Group, 99
Pesticides, 46, 48, 160
Petrochemical industry, 41-45

Philadelphia, 25, 132, 134, 193
Philippines, 8-9
Photovoltaic (solar) cells, 44, 104
Plastics recycling, 59, 97, 164, 169
"Pocketbook environmentalism," 85
Poland, 6, 113, 191
Pollution insurance, 55
"Prop 65", 32

R

Radon, 75, 80, 85, 98, 157-158
Reagan administration, 14, 243, 173-174
Real estate (and the environmental factor), 19, 20, 71-86
Recycling, 44, 97-98, 145-146, 164-169
"Red bag" waste, 69, 116, 147
Residential real estate, 72-86
Resource Conservation and Recovery Act (RCRA), 29, 31
Riedel Environmental Services, Inc., 88

S

S&L Crisis, 181
Safe Drinking Water Act, 30
Santiago (Chile), 9
Seattle, 165, 191
Shell Oil, 42
"Sick building syndrome", 27, 79, 155
Sierra Club, 82, 141
Sludge, 31, 166
Solar energy, 100-105
Solid waste disposal, 12, 75
Soviet Union, 5-6, 123, 180, 196

States and the environment, 28, 32-35
Steel-making, 59
Stocks (and the environmental factor), 87-108
"Strict retroactive liability," 54-55
Suntory International, 99
Superfund, 29, 81, 92, 182
Sustainable growth, 57

T

Tax Reform Act (of 1986) 15, 115, 116, 191
Tenneco, 42
Texas Eastern Corp., 42
Three Mile Island, 53
Timber, 48-49
Times Beach (Missouri), 20, 72, 73
Tourism (and the environment), 50-52
Trash collection costs, 12
Treasury Bonds, 112

U

Underground tanks (leaking), 35
Union Carbide, 44, 56
United Kingdom, 6, 7
United Nations, 11
University of Michigan, 151
Utilities (and the environment), 19, 52-53

V

Valdez oil spill, 11, 42, 49, 56
Vermont, 77
Virginia, 79
Volga River, 6

Index

W

Waste Management, Inc., 44,
  70, 88, 98
Waste-to-energy plants, 35
Westinghouse, 44
Weston, (Roy F., Inc.), 88, 91
Wharton School, 151
World Bank, 49

Y

Yale University, 151

Z

Zoning laws, 25, 85
Zurn Industries, 88